"The Object Lessons serie[s]
to magic: the books take
and animate them with a
political struggle, science
Filled with fascinating details and conveyed in sharp,
accessible prose, the books make the everyday world
come to life. Be warned: once you've read a few of these,
you'll start walking around your house, picking up
random objects, and musing aloud: 'I wonder what the
story is behind this thing?'"

Steven Johnson, author of *Where Good Ideas
Come From* and *How We Got to Now*

"Object Lessons describes themselves as 'short, beautiful
books,' and to that, I'll say, amen. . . . If you read enough
Object Lessons books, you'll fill your head with plenty
of trivia to amaze and annoy your friends and loved
ones—caution recommended on pontificating on the
objects surrounding you. More importantly, though
. . . they inspire us to take a second look at parts of
the everyday that we've taken for granted. These are
not so much lessons about the objects themselves,
but opportunities for self-reflection and storytelling.
They remind us that we are surrounded by a wondrous
world, as long as we care to look."

John Warner, *The Chicago Tribune*

"Besides being beautiful little hand-sized objects themselves, showcasing exceptional writing, the wonder of these books is that they exist at all . . . Uniformly excellent, engaging, thought-provoking, and informative."

Jennifer Bort Yacovissi, *Washington Independent Review of Books*

". . . edifying and entertaining . . . perfect for slipping in a pocket and pulling out when life is on hold."

Sarah Murdoch, *Toronto Star*

"[W]itty, thought-provoking, and poetic . . . These little books are a page-flipper's dream."

John Timpane, *The Philadelphia Inquirer*

"For my money, Object Lessons is the most consistently interesting nonfiction book series in America."

Megan Volpert, *PopMatters*

"Though short, at roughly 25,000 words apiece, these books are anything but slight."

Marina Benjamin, *New Statesman*

The joy of the series, of reading *Remote Control, Golf Ball, Driver's License, Drone, Silence, Glass, Refrigerator, Hotel,* and *Waste* . . . in quick succession, lies in encountering the various turns through which each of their authors has been put by his or her object . . . The object predominates, sits squarely center stage, directs the action. The object decides the genre, the chronology, and the limits of the study. Accordingly, the author has to take her cue from the *thing* she chose or that chose her. The result is a wonderfully uneven series of books, each one a *thing* unto itself."

Julian Yates, *Los Angeles Review of Books*

The Object Lessons series has a beautifully simple premise. Each book or essay centers on a specific object. This can be mundane or unexpected, humorous or politically timely. Whatever the subject, these descriptions reveal the rich worlds hidden under the surface of things."

Christine Ro, *Book Riot*

. . . a sensibility somewhere between Roland Barthes and Wes Anderson."

Simon Reynolds, **author of** *Retromania: Pop Culture's Addiction to Its Own Past*

OBJECT LESSONS

A book series about the hidden lives of ordinary things.

Series Editors:

Ian Bogost and Christopher Schaberg

In association with

BOOKS IN THE SERIES

blue jeans

CAROLYN PURNELL

BLOOMSBURY ACADEMIC

NEW YORK • LONDON • OXFORD • NEW DELHI • SYDNEY

BLOOMSBURY ACADEMIC
Bloomsbury Publishing Inc
1385 Broadway, New York, NY 10018, USA
50 Bedford Square, London, WC1B 3DP, UK
29 Earlsfort Terrace, Dublin 2, Ireland

BLOOMSBURY, BLOOMSBURY ACADEMIC and the Diana logo are
trademarks of Bloomsbury Publishing Plc

First published in the United States of America 2023

Cover design: Alice Marwick

Bloomsbury Publishing Inc does not have any control over, or responsibility for,
any third-party websites referred to or in this book. All internet addresses given
in this book were correct at the time of going to press. The author and publisher
regret any inconvenience caused if addresses have changed or sites have
ceased to exist, but can accept no responsibility for any such changes.

Library of Congress Cataloging-in-Publication Data
Names: Purnell, Carolyn, author.
Title: Blue jeans / Carolyn Purnell.
Description: New York: Bloomsbury Academic, 2023. | Series: Object lessons |
Includes bibliographical references and index. | Summary: "Blue jeans
may seem suited to every occasion, but their one-size-fits all appearance
hides a history of contradictions"– Provided by publisher.
Identifiers: LCCN 2022023776 (print) | LCCN 2022023777 (ebook) |
ISBN 9781501383748 (PB) | ISBN 9781501383755 (eBook) | ISBN 9781501383731
(ePDF) | ISBN 9781501383762
Subjects: LCSH: Jeans (Clothing)–History. | Fashion–United States–History. |
Clothing and dress–Social aspects.
Classification: LCC GT2085 .P87 2023 (print) | LCC GT2085 (ebook) |
DDC 391.00973–dc23/eng/20220520
LC record available at https://lccn.loc.gov/2022023776
LC ebook record available at https://lccn.loc.gov/2022023777

ISBN: PB: 978-1-5013-8374-8
ePDF: 978-1-5013-8373-1
eBook: 978-1-5013-8375-5

Series: Object Lessons

Typeset by Deanta Global Publishing Services, Chennai, India
Printed and bound in the United States of America

To find out more about our authors and books visit www.bloomsbury.com and
sign up for our newsletters.

For Diffan

CONTENTS

FIGURES

INTRODUCTION

THE MOST VERSATILE GARMENT

Between 1952 and 1976, my maternal grandmother worked at the Blue Buckle Overall Company, running pieces of coarse denim through a sewing machine. The needles had to be extra sharp in order to make it through the tough seams. One of the hardest parts, though, was the hot heaviness of the air and the thick, chemical smell of the dyed fabric. Tumbleweeds of blue cotton dust flew around the factory floor, and although supervisors warned workers to be careful about breathing it in, asthma was a common complaint. My grandfather serviced the machinery, making sure everything ran smoothly. He stooped over commercial equipment with needles that moved like hummingbird wings, greasing parts and tightening screws. Each night, my grandparents returned home with pricked fingers, hers stained blue and his oil black.

Blue jeans were almost as important to my father's family. They were in the cattle business, and every day, the men would tuck their jeans into their boots and push through briar-laden brush to fetch stray calves, mend broken fences, or check food troughs. T-shirts came and went, but jeans were harder to come by, and they were one of the most important parts of the ranch uniform. After all, snakes have a harder time biting through denim.

For my dad, Wranglers were the brand of choice because everyone knew they were built to last. Mud-smeared, blood-splattered, or sweat-soaked, those jeans could withstand everything farm life had to offer. This was a lesson I learned early on. In fact, I can remember church sermons from my childhood where the preacher urged the congregation to strive for a "blue jeans" relationship with Jesus—familiar, comfortable, durable, and daily. It baffled me why someone would equate what they believed to be the mightiest power in the universe with the humblest, dirtiest garments I knew. Now, though, I understand that blue jeans are nothing if not an exercise in opposites.

While the United States has accepted jeans as a symbol of American culture, today, jeans are a global good. On worldwide average, people wear jeans at least three days a week, and more than half of people say they enjoy wearing them.[1] Every year, new consumers take the denim plunge, and the global jeans market is expected to grow from $73.09 billion in 2020 to $102.45 billion in 2025, with the fastest growth in Asia.[2] By 2023, China will become the largest consumer of denim in the world.[3] Blue jeans' production has gone equally global. Denim mills in China, Pakistan, and India churn out fabric dyed with synthetic indigo from Germany and Brazil. Factory workers in Vietnam, Hong Kong, and Japan cut, sew, and hem so exporters can ship the products worldwide.

Jeans have a reputation for being comfortable, but unless you're dealing with jeggings (a portmanteau of jeans and leggings) or a pair of jeans made with pre-washed or elasticized fabric, there's a "breaking in" period before the stiff cloth relents. That toughness was a selling point when Levi Strauss made blue jeans in the 1870s to withstand the hard work of mining, but now, jeans have become the epitome of leisure. Most consumers still prefer jeans made primarily of cotton, but they don't want the old-fashioned, stiff denim.[4] They crave softer, washed cloth or stretchier textile blends made with synthetic fibers. The workhorse of the closet has been consigned to Casual Friday.

In the 1950s, celebrities like James Dean transformed the utilitarian clothing of industrial labor into a glamorous statement of youthful rebellion. From there, it wasn't a far leap for this humble garment to the hautest of fashion runways. "I have often said that I wish I had invented blue jeans," Yves Saint Laurent mused in 1983.[5] He may not have invented blue jeans, but Saint Laurent certainly found a high-end market for them. At the time of writing, a pair of men's straight-fit jeans in "dirty winter blue" costs $950 on the YSL website.[6] Luxury jeans may look virtually the same as workaday Wranglers, but the cultural and economic signals they send are worlds apart.

Blue jeans also pull a masterful sleight of hand when it comes to weathering the tides of fashion. Jeans masquerade as a timeless article of clothing, but in reality, jean styles come and go as quickly as other fashion trends. Shopping for jeans can be enough to give even the most veteran shoppers decision fatigue. There are casual jeans and dressy jeans; cheap jeans and expensive jeans; jeans for women who want a "boyfriend" cut and jeans that earn male wearers the loaded label of "metrosexual." Jeans are the clothes that help you fit in, but as generations of hippies, skaters, punks, and hip-hop enthusiasts can tell you, they just as easily help you stand out.

The contradictions continue . . . For some, blue might be a color associated with comfort, leisure, and freedom. What could be easier than slipping into a soft, friendly pair of jeans that has faded to the color of a summer sky? But for many people around the world, blue was and is a color of oppression. The modern indigo industry was created by the British East India Company, and capitalists' treatment of colonial indigo workers was so severe it led to a prolonged series of riots known as the Blue Mutiny. Jeans are a canonical symbol of American identity, but they also bear the legacy of a bleak chapter in the United States' history. For more than a century, thousands of African and Indigenous slaves suffered to bring indigo dye to the masses. Today, the brutality of blue continues as low-wage textile workers grapple with the harmful effects of the toxic chemicals they work with daily.

But the meaning of blue jeans has proved so flexible that even their bloody legacy has been subverted and refashioned. Jeans' manufacturing may have gone hand-in-hand with oppressive power structures, but during the twentieth century, the finished garment became a symbol of resistance. In the 1960s, young Black women activists reclaimed denim and mobilized blue jeans as a symbol in the fight for civil rights. Members of the Student Nonviolent Coordinating Committee stepped onstage at the March on Washington wearing denim jeans, overalls, and skirts as a sign of solidarity with African-American sharecroppers and a rejection of "respectable" Black middle-class complacency.[7] Recent protests in India and Italy have harnessed the symbolic power of jeans, and over the last few decades, activist organizations have used denim to raise awareness about issues like sexual violence, domestic abuse, and government corruption. Jeans may seem like uncontroversial garments, but in certain contexts, they've been nothing short of revolutionary.

In essence, jeans are the perfect emblem for opposing values. Over the course of one hundred and fifty years, they have become a universal signifier, ready to fit any context, meaning, and body. The layers of contradictions surrounding jeans have grown so dense that they've become invisible. Jeans are, at once, a garment that means everything and nothing. This invisibility makes jeans perfectly suited to modernity, given that so many aspects of modern life have been streamlined, homogenized, and globalized in the name of efficiency and convenience. You're as likely to see a pair of 501s in Dubai as Dubuque.

Everyone's acquainted with blue jeans, so it's easy to assume that there's not much to really *know* about them. But don't be fooled. Behind that superficial layer of anonymity, there's a whole world of meaning. Sometimes, the most invisible, anonymous objects can be the richest of all.

1 DISTRESS

Several mornings a week, my father meets a few of his friends at the edge of a country road for a walk. Over the course of a mile, they pass sweeping, cattle-filled fields while they share the latest local news and laugh over schoolboy antics. Every now and then, they'll discuss a particularly juicy bit of gossip—who called the sheriff over a rowdy neighbor's gun practice, who bagged the biggest deer, and who they think is "all hat, no cattle" (full of BS). By the end of the walk, they've worked up a sweat and have tabs on the whole neighborhood.

One morning, I was lucky enough to snag an invitation to this exclusive club. About halfway down the road, my dad announced that I was writing a book about blue jeans, and the flood began. "Oh, so you're going to talk about how the Levi's 501s changed everything . . . And then how Wrangler pushed into the rodeo market in the 40s. Man, those were some good jeans. Did you know . . ." And so it continued. By the time we reached the end of the walk, I had learned why Cinch jeans were the local denim du jour, why the button fly gave way to zippers, and how Japanese jean-fans helped turn secondhand Levi's into big-ticket collectibles.

9 Beating a vat by hand.

FIGURE 1.1 The world's most comfortable garment has a less-than-comfortable history. This photo by Oscar Mallitte shows workers beating a vat of indigo in Allahabad, India in 1877. Digital image courtesy of the Getty's Open Content Program.

I grew up around cattle ranchers, bull riders, and farmers, so I know how important jeans are in their daily lives. But until that morning, I don't think I understood just how deep the culture of blue jeans actually runs. At that point, I had been researching blue jeans for months, yet these men casually knew the historical timeline better than I did. And they weren't the only ones. Everywhere I went around my small East Texas hometown, when someone learned about my book's topic, they became a fount of knowledge.

"Remember when rodeo clowns started wearing jeans with ads on the butt?"

"Gunslingers wore sashes 'cause they didn't have loops to hold their britches up."

"I read about a guy who hunts for denim in old mines. He sells it for a pretty penny!"[1]

After a number of these conversations, it struck me that rural folks—or at least the ones in my life—have an almost intrinsic knowledge of blue jeans. They've never made a study of the subject, but somehow, they know the ins and outs of jeans and why, when, and how certain styles came into their lives.

The average person on the street may not be able to tell you that Levi Strauss got the patent for riveting pants in 1873, or that 1947 was the year the Blue Bell Overall Company launched a jeans line for cowboys (Wrangler). But almost every person has a story to tell about blue jeans. They know about the bell bottoms of the 1970s, or they can remember when skinny jeans took the world by storm around 2005. Most people also have deeply personal associations with blue jeans. I remember wearing my favorite pair of jeans on a date before realizing, much later, that there was a giant hole in the backside. I recall my mixed feelings about making the move from the juniors' section to women's sizes and how, in middle school, the cool kids used Sharpies to draw on each other's pants legs. We're all amateur historians when it comes to blue jeans.

Whether they're the garment you love to live in or the one you hate to try on, blue jeans are familiar to each and every one of us. But for the most part, their backstory remains a mystery. Levi Strauss tends to get most of the credit for their creation, but by the time Levi's signature jeans hit the market, many of their features were already standard among work trousers. The Levi's website carefully reminds customers, "We did not invent the cut or fit of the waist overalls; what we did was take traditional men's work pants and rivet them."[2] Blue jeans have a longer history, reaching back well before the Gold Rush put Strauss on his path to workwear fame.

According to the *Oxford English Dictionary*, the word "jean" was already in use by 1567.[3] So, if we want to get to the real source of these beloved trousers, we must push back to at least the sixteenth century. But as is the case with many commonplace objects, the further back we go, the hazier the history becomes. Over time, the origin story of jeans has become a tangled skein of allegation, lore, and urban legend. One thing we do know is that blue jeans are as American as apple pie—which is to say, not really American at all. (The earliest apple pie recipes date from medieval England.)

Instead of a single origin story for blue jeans, we have a constellation of narratives. The development of workmen's trousers, "jean" fabric, and denim all have their own lore, as do the iconic features of cinched waists, suspender buttons, back pockets, and everything else that came together to make blue jeans blue jeans. This meandering history could send even the most intrepid historian down a never-ending series of rabbit holes. Consequently, the following narrative contains only some of the most essential threads, in their most widely accepted versions, to explain how one of the world's most treasured garments came into being.

Centuries ago, workers in the Indian village of Dongri produced a coarse, brown cotton cloth with a reputation for being hard-wearing and reliable. During the European Age of Exploration, Western traders were especially taken with this so-called "dungaree" cloth, which became a popular option for boat sails. Once the sails had seen their fair share of the salt and sea, the ships' mariners repurposed the tattered pieces into work trousers.[4] These piecemeal garments probably looked a fright, but that scarcely mattered to sailors seeking protection from the harsh elements. During their journeys, many of these dungaree-clad sailors found their way to the Italian city of Genoa, which was one of the most powerful ports in the world. Word spread about the miraculously durable Indian fabric, and soon, traders started selling Dongri's namesake textile at a hefty markup.

As the popularity of dungaree and its affiliated trousers grew, consumers clamored for a cheaper alternative. During the sixteenth century, enterprising Genoese manufacturers decided to make their own utilitarian cloth. Producers sprang up across Genoa, or as the city was known in French, Gênes. Soon, the wealthy port city boasted an equally wealthy trade in this new, sturdy cotton fabric. English traders, apparently unable or unwilling to say Genoa or Gênes, simply called the textile "jean."

During the early modern era, France was the beating heart of the European textile trade, and the success of jean cloth must have been galling to hyper-competitive French manufacturers. Not wanting to be outdone by the Genoese, French producers quickly devised their own hardy cloth. In the southeastern city of Nîmes, a cotton-wool blend known as "serge de Nîmes" soon poured from the looms. Once again, English tongues craved a simpler version, so the fabric's name was shortened to "denim."

At their inception, jean and denim were distinct fabrics. Both were woven with two threads—warp and woof—but jean was made with two threads of the same color. Denim required one dyed thread and one white thread, which explains why the interior of most jeans today is lighter than the exterior. Over time, the slight difference between the two cloths shaded into an inconsequential bit of trivia, and "jeans" came to refer to the style of trousers, while "denim" referred to the fabric.[5]

It took another few centuries before the United States entered the story with denim-clad cowboys and Levi Strauss' distinctive miner pants. But before jeans could become an American icon—and, in turn, a truly global good—they had to undergo a major transformation. Namely, they had to become blue.

Blue Blood

Marshall, the small East Texas town where I grew up, is built on a foundation of thick red and white clay, but it was blue that helped fuel the economy. In 1895, the Kentucky businessman W. F. Rocker moved there with a plan to turn the earth into art, and what began as a fledgling enterprise became one of the largest pottery businesses in America. Over the years, Rocker and his successors, the Ellis family, produced a wide range of pottery goods, the most distinctive of which were churns, pots, and jugs the color of raw cream, streaked with rich cobalt blue.

Many of these hand-turned pieces are collector's items today, but when I was growing up, almost every family had a bowl, mug, or pot emblazoned with the signature blue stripes and Marshall Pottery stamp. During school tours, we watched as artists dabbed and dotted the clay, creating watery trails destined to become fire-hardened permanence. Some kids took home pottery with their names, while others wanted pieces decorated with rabbits or flowers. My favorite mug, which I still use, bears a ring of cobalt barbed wire around the top.

Even to children, that blue felt like magic, like a color that had been plucked from the nighttime sky and stamped onto clay. A gift taken from the gods, in the same way Prometheus stole fire and handed it to awe-struck humans. The allure of that blue always contained a hint of danger, even if none of us, as schoolchildren, could put our finger on it. As an adult, I've learned that in unskilled hands, cobalt blue was a color that could kill. The word cobalt comes from German folklore surrounding *kobold*, a type of sprite that torments and poisons miners.[6] A kobold's favorite hiding place was smaltite, an ore that forms brilliant blue crystals laced with deadly arsenic. During the nineteenth century, chemists learned how to create cobalt without sacrificing lives to the deadly "cobalt bloom" of mines, but death would forever lurk in the pigment's past.

A few miles away from Marshall Pottery, the Blue Buckle jeans factory also loomed large over our childish imaginations. By the time I was in school, the factory had closed down, but the hulking, abandoned building was a daily sight, perched downtown near the public library and the Methodist church. Many of us had family members who remembered the flurry of blue cotton and the intensity of sewing in the Texas heat. Our town was filled with memories of callused fingers, blue sputum, and legs stiff from standing. Still, most of these stories were delivered in a matter-of-fact "that's just how it was" tone, not with any sense that things should have been different. Because these were stories we all shared. Whether your family was connected to pottery or jeans, it was almost inevitable that if you had lived in Marshall long enough, somehow, somewhere, blue was in your blood.

Marshall's magic blue wasn't just a visual delight. It also meant money. It meant having a roof over your head and clothes on your body. That single color kept local families fed for generations, and Marshall wasn't alone in its blue-bound livelihood. For millennia, blue has been such an attention-grabbing hue that its production has fueled cities, industries, and empires. And the rarer the blue, the higher the price.

In nature, blue is a relatively uncommon color. Yes, the sky and the sea may be blue, but these are immaterial tricks of light, not tangible substances that can be fixed on canvas or cloth. Today, I can jaunt to a paint store and have someone mix up a pot of delicious liquid blue in minutes, so it's easy to forget how recently humans acquired such a rare privilege. For much of history, people only had access to the colorants they found in the world around them—the plants, animals, and minerals from which they could extract delight. Before mass transportation and a far-reaching system of globalized trade, most people relied on the limited palette of their local lands.

In Europe, few of these regional treasures produced blue pigments or dyes. The most consistent source of blue was woad, *Isatis tinctoria*, a weedy plant with yellow flowers. To store woad, one collected the leaves, rolled them into large onion-sized balls, and dried them in the open air. Then, to produce blue dye, the balls were soaked in urine under the hot sun for three days. The remaining yellow liquid could then be used to dye textiles, which would turn blue after they were removed from the dye bath and hung to dry in the oxygen-rich air.[7] Woad blue was one of nature's most glorious (albeit smelly) magic tricks.

Woad had been cultivated in Europe as far back as Anglo-Saxon and Viking times; by the thirteenth century, it had become a major industry across western Europe. Governments raked in tidy profits by levying steep taxes on every stage of production.[8] In England, woad became so valuable that it was handed down in wills, and dyers often held prominent civic positions. In France and Germany, woad merchants displayed their immense wealth by building opulent houses, and the ever-enterprising Genoese merchants made a mint transporting woad across Europe's maritime trade routes.[9] Europeans had steady access to woad blue, but high demand often meant high prices.

Plus, woad had several material limitations. It contains the dye chemical indigo, but the plant has a low dye content. Woad colorants are not as intensely blue or color-fast as the indigo produced by the *Indigofera tinctoria* plant, which grows well in tropical and subtropical regions (and therefore isn't native to Europe). Woad also had another major tick in its "cons" column. It's a nitrogen-hungry plant that releases large quantities of ammonia. It depletes the soil, leaving wasteland in its wake, whereas *Indigofera tinctoria* is a soil-replenishing legume.

Where woad falls short, *Indigofera tinctoria* excels. It's sumptuous in all its shades—from coy, retreating sky to foreboding, magnetic ink. It's a blue that radiates and tantalizes. It can call to you in your sleep. In pre-modern Europe, even the lowest quality *Indigofera* indigo could command a formidable price because that kind of true, deep, dazzling, *dizzying* blue was a luxury. It belonged only to the social elite who could afford the rarest, brightest colors from foreign lands. In fact, the name of another famous blue, ultramarine, means "from beyond the sea," and the pigment that bore this name was staggeringly expensive. The source of ultramarine was the mineral lapis lazuli, which was mined almost exclusively in Afghanistan for six thousand years. Once the raw material had been hewn from mountain crags, it journeyed on donkeys' backs to expert pigment-makers who toiled to extract the mineral's purest essence, grind it, and knead it into a wax and resin paste using a specialized chemical solution. One hundred grams of lapis lazuli produced only four grams of pigment.[10] By the time the labor-intensive colorant sailed across the ocean, reached Europe's shores, and traveled to other markets, its price reached astronomical heights.

Throughout the Middle Ages, pure blue was not the common color of a hard-working, casual garment. It was a status symbol, suitable for only the most skilled artists and artisans, wealthiest patrons, and holiest subjects, like Virgin Mary, the mother of God. Any peasant could see blue and perhaps find fleeting traces of it in their gardens, but to truly possess the hue, one needed blue blood. No wonder, then, that people at all social levels yearned for the color. It was beautiful, to be sure, but blue also bore the remarkable weight of respect and power.

As Europeans extended their colonial reach into other, warmer parts of the globe, indigo became one of the most coveted commodities. The European appetite for indigo blue seemed insatiable, and merchants and producers scrambled to increase the supply. Through ever-deepening systems of colonialism and slavery, commercial quantities of indigo began to reach Europe's shores in the seventeenth century, and landowners cultivated indigo at a rate that would have been unheard of a century earlier.[11]

To say that blue had become cheap by the eighteenth century would be an overstatement, especially given its wild price fluctuations, contingent on everything from war and weevils to precipitation and pirates. But with the expansion of indigo cultivation, blue was finally within reach for the aspirational masses. People of all classes embraced blue with abandon. Curtains, clothing, pottery, furniture—homes were filled with blue, blue, and more blue. Tradesmen wore blue aprons, making them easy to pick out of a crowd. Everything from sugar to starch was wrapped in blue paper.[12] Armies across Europe and America donned blue uniforms, keeping indigo in high demand, and sailors became known for their characteristic "navy blue" garb.

Hands down, blue became the favorite color of European society from the eighteenth century onward.[13] Indigo was such a staple that by 1815, Bengal was sending 7,650,000 pounds of indigo to eager Londoners each year.[14] Bengal was one of Britain's most important indigo territories, but it was by no means its only one, nor was Britain the only European power to undertake the trade. Throughout the global economy, the cultivation of blue was a big business. What was once the rarest color in Europe quickly became one of the most ubiquitous. It retained many of its older associations—peace, quality, honor, and constancy— but it no longer connoted wealth. The exclusive color of aristocratic portraits and heraldry became the common color of blood-stained butchers' aprons and trash-heap sugar wrappers.

By 1890, even the word "blue" had become more common. In his dictionary of colloquial speech, the English lexicographer John Stephen Farmer noted, "Few words enter more largely into the composition of slang and colloquialisms bordering on slang than does the word BLUE."[15] Sure enough, the subsequent twelve pages of definitions proves it. The verb "to blue" could mean to blush, pawn, spend, miscalculate, or steal. "Flying the blue pigeon," meant taking lead from the roofs of houses. To "blue one's screw" was to squander one's salary. A "blue funk" meant feeling so nervous or frightened that one began to stink, while "to look blue" meant to be astonished or annoyed. A "blue dahlia" referred to something rare and coveted, while a "blue boy" was an abscess typically associated with venereal disease (much less coveted). To "make the air blue" meant to curse or swear, and "blue stone" or "blue ruin" were the types of rot-gut gin best left to "blued" (a.k.a., drunk) folk. Literary ladies were called bluestockings, and bullets were known as blue plums, blue pills, or blue whistlers.

Farmer was astounded, not only by the wide variety of slang involving the color blue but also by the wide range in connotations. Blue, he marveled, was "expressive alike of the utmost contempt, as of all that men hold dearest and love best," and he could discern no pattern in how the word was used. "As far as the evidence is concerned," he explained, "both the good and bad shades of meaning appear to run contemporaneously."[16] In essence, blue had come to mean all things to all people. It was neither rich nor poor, good nor evil, high nor low, precisely because it was *all* of those things. How fitting, then, that the most contradictory color became a key component of one of the world's most contradictory garments.

According to a wide range of color preference surveys, blue still reigns supreme. Regardless of gender, geography, or political persuasion, a majority of people across the globe identify it as their favorite.[17] The psychologists Stephen E. Palmer and Karen Schloss suggest that people prefer blue because most of the things we associate with it, like the sky or water, have positive connotations.[18] But the historian Michel Pastoureau suggests that the reason may have more to do with neutrality than positivity: "When we declare that our favorite color is blue, after all, what do we really reveal about ourselves? Nothing, or almost nothing, because the response is so predictable . . . In Western color symbolism [blue] doesn't make waves, but is calm, pacified, distant, almost neutral."[19] In Pastoureau's estimation, blue is so inoffensive, it has almost become meaningless.

That's the closest I've come to understanding why blue jeans deviate from normal color rules. Today, few people remember the old standard "blue and green should never be seen," a color rule asserting that blue and green clash and should therefore never appear in tandem. A generation of color experts, interior designers, and fashion experts have pushed back against this rule, insisting that it's old-fashioned.[20] Yet, even when fashionistas still lived by this precept, denim seemed to be an exception. A green shirt wouldn't clash with jeans, even though there was no denying that jeans are blue. Likewise, when I was growing up, I always heard that one shouldn't wear blue with black (especially navy blue); yet somehow, navy jeans and a black shirt are a perfectly acceptable combination. No one bats an eye. Blue jeans have become so commonplace that most people don't even register them as blue. They're a neutral that goes with everything. When it comes to jeans, what was once the world's most coveted color is now practically invisible.

Blue Dye

Indigo may have taken Europe by storm in the seventeenth and eighteenth centuries, but other parts of the globe have recognized its value for millennia. The earliest definitive archaeological findings reveal that indigo was already in use in South America by the fifth millennium BCE.[21] Remarkably, these fragments have retained their blue color because indigo is one of the hardiest natural dyes. It fades, but unlike many other colorants, it never changes hue. Indigo blue, it seems, stays blue until the end of time.

Ancient Egyptian dyers inserted blue stripes into linen mummy cloths. The Bible mentions blue textiles, and ancient civilizations in Central and South America had a firm grasp on indigo dyeing. In Indonesia, there's evidence that indigo had been introduced by the end of the first millennium BCE, along with the Sanskrit word *nila* (referring to both the indigo plant and dark blue). The word indigo itself comes from the Greek word *indikon*, meaning a substance from India. This etymology reveals how widely indigo had already traveled in antiquity.[22]

A Liberian myth tells of a woman who ate a piece of the sky and floated into blissful dreams. While she was asleep, her baby rolled off its bed of leaves and smothered in the tall grass. When the woman woke, she knew she had been punished for her temerity. She cradled her baby and fell unconscious with grief. In her dreams, the water spirits revealed that mixing salty tears, urine, river water, ash, and wild indigo leaves would create the vivid blue she had craved. This woman went on to share the secret of indigo dyeing with her people, and High God pulled the sky higher up, so no one else would be tempted to eat it.[23]

In many cultures, indigo dyers were revered because theirs was a finicky craft. Indigo produces beautiful color, but it doesn't yield its secrets as readily as other natural dyes. Some natural dyestuffs are substantive, meaning that all you need is heat to get them to stick to a fiber. Turmeric is a great example. Toss some turmeric into boiling water with wool, and you'll see glorious golden results. But most dyestuffs are adjective, meaning that you have to add a chemical substance called a mordant to make them stick to the fibers. (The word mordant comes from the Old French word for bite, so think of a mordant as the stuff that helps dye sink its teeth into fabric.) Most homemakers knew how to place flowers and herbs into vats with a pinch of alum to get beautiful colors to hold fast.

Indigo is a different animal altogether. It doesn't need a mordant, but dyeing with indigo also isn't quite so easy as adding heat. First, dyers add bundles of indigo leaves to a vat filled with warm alkaline water. They weigh the leaves down with logs or stones to make sure they're submerged and leave the liquid to ferment.[24] Any number of substances can be added to speed up this fermentation and maintain the alkalinity of the brew. Common additions include ash, lime, honey, liquor, animal droppings, and stale urine.[25] Once the dye has been drawn out of the leaves, the liquid turns yellowish-green, topped with a glistening coppery film. At this point, cloth can be dipped into the vat, but the dye is weak. It takes successive dipping to build up a deep, dark color, and, much to the dismay of early modern European traders, the liquid was difficult to transport.[26]

To make indigo into a commercial powerhouse, traders needed to fully extract the pigment so it could be easily moved. Indians discovered the necessary techniques in antiquity, but European colonists put the process on steroids by turning it into a veritable factory system. Once the indigo leaves reached the desired level of fermentation, the liquid was drained into a second tank, and lime was added. Then the hard work began. Standing inside the tank, workers energetically stirred the water with hefty wooden paddles. As the liquid oxidized, a foamy blue froth rose to the surface, while solid particles sank to the bottom of the vat. Layer by painstaking layer, workers skimmed the clear liquid off, until eventually, only a dense blue sludge remained. This sediment was then spread out on cloths and partially dried in the sun. While it was still pliable, the paste was molded into cakes, which were then baked into hard lumps of pigment.[27]

Prepared this way, indigo was ideal for long-distance trade. It wouldn't rot, spill, or take up excess space in a cargo hold. These highly concentrated lumps were so potent and profitable, they came to be known as blue-gold. Back in Europe, far removed from the painstaking labor that went into producing indigo, many people assumed these bricks were the pigment's natural form. A 1616 English dictionary defined indigo as "a stone brought out of Turkey."[28]

These blue bricks may have put an end to traders' material difficulties carrying indigo across the globe, but its meteoric rise in Europe still wasn't a forgone conclusion. When indigo entered the European market, woad producers were far from happy that a new blue was encroaching on their territory. Wealthy landowners and merchants with colonial interests duked it out with those firmly rooted on the metropole's soil, and the battle was fierce. Woad producers turned out to be good lobbyists. All across Europe, they persuaded the public that indigo was "the devil's dye" and that it was poisonous. Woad advocates in the Netherlands warned that anyone who handled indigo would become sexually impotent; in the Languedoc province of France, the king banned the import of indigo in 1598 and decreed that anyone found using the "deceitful" dye would be sentenced to death.[29]

Despite this smear campaign, producers and consumers alike realized that indigo was a superior substance, and demand for the foreign plant mounted. By the eighteenth century, dyers began to take their chances bypassing indigo laws. It didn't take long for governments to see that they could fill their coffers more quickly with the profits of indigo than those of woad, and the woeful woad producers were, by and large, left out in the cold.

Indigo's fortunes also went hand-in-hand with another major cash crop: cotton. While it's possible to dye cotton with woad, the color doesn't take as well to plant fibers as it does to protein fibers like wool or silk. Indigo, though, is well suited to cotton, which doesn't easily absorb most natural dyes. And during the seventeenth and eighteenth centuries, cotton was becoming *big* business for Europeans. For centuries, cotton production had centered in China and India, with little interest or intervention from Europe. But once European entrepreneurs learned how useful and lucrative the "fabric of our lives" could be, they set their sights on the humble fiber.

The historian Sven Beckert has meticulously charted how cotton took center stage in European "war capitalism," an economic system built on slavery, imperial expansion, armed trade, and resources stolen from Indigenous peoples. "With increasing frequency," he explains "Europeans inserted themselves, often violently, into the global networks of the cotton trade."[30] Quickly, Europeans learned that the beautiful cotton textiles they could obtain from India appealed not only to other Europeans but also to Africans, Americans, and Asians. By 1760, Britain exported one-third of its cotton cloth, with Africa and America as its most important markets. By the end of the eighteenth century, that number had risen to two-thirds, and only fifty years later, it clocked in at a staggering 94 percent.[31] Europe's success in the textile trade helped cement their power across the globe.

The colonial system was stunning for its efficiency, economic success, and sheer cruelty. One British magistrate in Bengal testified before a legal commission, "Not a chest of indigo reached England without being stained with human blood."[32] But England wasn't the only country with blood on its hands. Portugal and Spain established indigo plantations in Central and South America, and other European nations quickly followed suit in tropical and subtropical regions around the world. The Dutch produced indigo in Indonesia, the British manufactured it in India, and the French and British set up large-scale operations in the Caribbean and parts of North America.[33]

In the United States, South Carolina was a major hub of indigo production. The dyestuff created there was of a lower quality than that produced in other parts of the world, but it was also cheaper, making it suitable for worker garments, military uniforms, clothing for slaves, everyday goods, and items to trade with American Indians.[34] At the peak of the indigo trade in 1775, the colony exported over 1.1 million pounds of indigo annually.[35] This number may not have a lot of meaning in the abstract, but consider it this way: it takes about one hundred pounds of plant material to produce a pound of the dyestuff.[36] So, to make a small indigo cake, it took up to 1,450 square feet of land.[37] That's larger than most American apartments. Think, now, of how much labor went into that single cake of blue—how many hands touched the plants from the time the seeds were sown to the time the blocks were placed on ships and sent to the far reaches of the earth. As the indigo trade grew, so did the seizure of Indigenous territory and the enslavement of Africans and American Indians. All those lives, all that land, distilled into a package that weighed less than a grapefruit.

The juggernaut of war capitalism, fueled by the twin luxuries of cotton and indigo, reconfigured the global economic system. By the time Levi Strauss and his business partner Jacob Davis opened their first factory in 1873, indigo-dyed cotton twill (denim) was an obvious choice for their hard-wearing, economical trousers. Cotton and indigo were a dream team, supported by an almost unfathomable scale of production. Indigo workers worldwide labored around the clock. The sickening odor of fermenting leaves and decomposing matter attracted swarming flies. Workers' muscles ached from churning the heavy liquid, their backs became hunched from repeated stooping, and their nails and skin bore blue stains that refused to fade. In India, workers resented the harsh conditions, but even more than their aching muscles, they resented the fact that they were forced to use their land to produce a colonial cash crop instead of the food supplies their communities needed. In 1859, indigo workers hit a breaking point and led a series of revolts that have been termed the Blue Mutiny.

Indian indigo farming worked on a contract basis. The farmer, or *ryot*, typically leased his land from a *zamindar* (landowner). British indigo planters used the zamindars as middlemen; the planters struck deals with the landowners, who then passed the expectations on to the ryots.[38] Ryots received advances for their work, which theoretically compensated them for their labor and materials, but the ryots had little say in the contracts' provisions. Landowners or planters often sent armed men to bully peasants into accepting unfavorable terms.[39] If a planter expected to receive a huge amount of indigo at the end of the season, it was the ryots' duty to produce it, and they had little room to argue or fight back.

Increasingly, ryots were forced to devote more and more land to indigo, squeezing out room for crops like rice and lentils, which kept their families alive. As if that weren't bad enough, years of scarcity further complicated the picture. If farmers had a bad crop and couldn't repay the advances, their debt carried over to the following year. Over time, the ryots' debts compounded, and there was no way for farmers to make the kind of profit that would get them out of the hole.[40] Most of the money from indigo went to the planters, not the farmers, and blue dye didn't do much for empty bellies.

In 1859, after five years of bad weather, the situation came to a head. Thousands of farmers refused to take advances, announcing that they had no intention of planting indigo. This mutiny swelled over the next couple of years to include nearly five million peasants throughout lower Bengal.[41] While the indigo revolts were largely passive and peaceful, there were places where a militant mood prevailed. In some areas, peasants destroyed the factories that produced the packed cakes of color. In others, planters tried to coerce the peasants, who fought back, refusing to be intimidated with violence.[42]

In 1860, the Lieutenant Governor of Bengal appointed an Indigo Commission to investigate the condition of the industry. The Commission's final report "revealed the existence of faults on both sides," but made the boundaries of the contracts clearer. If planters obtained agreements through fraud, force, or intimidation, farmers were not obligated to honor them.[43] Peace was gradually restored, but the truce was uneasy. Many planters moved their industry to other regions, and tensions continued to flare up between Indian indigo workers and planters for decades.[44] Famously, in 1916, the animosity escalated again, and a young activist named Mohandas Gandhi led the resistance.

While one type of blue mutiny occurred on the Indian subcontinent, another mutiny was taking place in continental Europe. Starting in the 1850s, chemists learned how to recreate the molecular structure of popular colorants using cheap, abundant materials like coal tar. Gone were the days of needing thousands of insects or tons of rock to make a single cake of pigment. Gone were the days of shipping precious colors across the sea, praying that they wouldn't succumb to rot, tempests, or thieves. With synthetic colorants, producers simply needed a few vats, some cheap and ready chemicals, and a steady supply of labor. The whole process could be carried out on domestic soil, without the slow time frame and expensive overhead that accompanied overseas production.

Thanks to the new chemical colors, European manufacturers could produce pigments, dyes, and vibrant products on an industrial scale. Colors that had only ever touched the bodies of nobles suddenly flooded the streets of Europe. Shopgirls could buy red shawls. Bakers could purchase green cravats. And seamstresses could wear electric purple stockings. The world was awash in vivid colors, the likes of which had never been seen—at least not in such quantities.

Yet, even in this new world of riotous colors, blue remained elusive. It resisted chemists at every turn, refusing to be synthesized in a cheaper, more widely accessible form. The indigo industry continued to thrive while other natural pigment industries faltered. In 1865, the German chemist Adolf von Baeyer figured out indigo's chemical structure, but it wasn't until 1897 that his employer, Badische Anilin Soda Fabrik (BASF) successfully released Indigo Pure, the first synthetic indigo. BASF had invested eighteen million gold marks to develop the product, which was more than the company was even worth at the time.[45]

That risky investment paid off beyond their wildest dreams. BASF's success as a dye manufacturer allowed the company to expand into other products. Today, they are the largest chemical producer in the world, and BASF's sister company Bayer is one of the largest pharmaceutical companies. BASF was an innovator in the production of sulfuric acid, ammonia-based fertilizers, rubber, and fuels. One of the company's subsidiaries even came up with the first tape recorder in 1935. But not all of BASF's innovations have been salutary. Their sister company IG Farben produced Zyklon-B, the lethal gas used in Nazi concentration camps during World War II, and twenty-three of the company's directors were tried for war crimes during the Nuremberg trials. All of BASF's successes—and iniquities—stemmed from the successes of Indigo Pure, and on a deeper level, the public's hunger for blue.

Blue is a powerful color. It does not sit idly by. Instead, it has quietly reached its fingers into virtually every aspect of human life, asserting itself with beauty, majesty, and terror. For thousands of years, humans have sought to harness blue, and beginning in the early modern era, Europeans began to do so with alarming success. A blanket of blue washing across continents might sound lovely, but that beautiful hue came at a high human cost. What's the real price that we've paid for having blue on demand?

Blue Is Not Green

By the 1920s, natural dyes constituted less than 10 percent of the worldwide market for colorants.[46] Synthetic dyes like

Indigo Pure marked the way of the future, and today, they are the predominant source of blue jeans' iconic color.

Indigo, including synthetic indigo, isn't water soluble, so it doesn't seep into cotton fully. The core of a blue-dyed cotton thread will always stay white, and with every wash, a bit more blue will loosen its hold on the fibers. This might be seen as a shortcoming, but many denim-lovers say this is precisely what makes blue jeans so special. Jeans change with their owners, losing color, softening, and taking shape with each successive wear. It's easy to develop a relationship with such a garment. As you and your jeans mold to each other, you form a kind of symbiosis.

If that sounds like a beautiful relationship to have with an object, it is. But in reality, many consumers don't keep their jeans long enough to develop that connection. Or, they purchase so many jeans that no single pair reaches the "lived-in" point. On average, U.S. women own six pairs of jeans and men own five.[47] In Mexico, the average number leaps to sixteen pairs, and in China, more than half of consumers say they buy denim with short seasonal lifecycles to keep up with the latest trends.[48]

Many of us are familiar with the concept of fast fashion, which involves producing trendy, inexpensive clothing at lightning speed. You may also be aware of the toll that fast fashion takes on laborers and the environment. But before researching this book, I didn't realize that denim is one of fast fashion's most pernicious culprits. It's extremely energy-, land-, water-, and chemical-intensive to produce. Denim is a resource-hungry beast, which we willingly feed more and more with each passing year. Leaving aside the amount of water it takes to produce cotton (which is itself a water-intensive product with a huge carbon footprint), it can take up to 2,900 gallons of water to make a single pair of jeans.[49]

Dyeing blue jeans requires building up the color over a series of successive dips. To reach the desired level of saturation, cotton can be dipped up to twelve times. In her book *Fugitive Denim,* journalist Rachel Louise Snyder describes her visit to the dye room at Legler, one of Italy's oldest textile firms:

> The process requires a series of connected dye boxes and machines more than a football field in length that move tens of thousands of yarns per second into and out of the indigo vats. At Legler, an indigo vat or dye box is about the size of a small car, and the indigo inside it froths and bubbles and gurgles, reeking suspiciously of overheated molding cheese. The vats operate, like much of the rest of the manufacturing side of the company, twenty-four hours a day in three shifts, five days a week.[50]

These vast vats and successive dips create an enormous amount of wastewater, which typically can't be cleaned or reused thanks to dye chemicals. Sulfur dyes, which are a cheap and popular tool for creating a vintage denim look, are especially dangerous, and the chemical residue remains in water, even after treatment.[51]

In addition to dyeing, a denim thread often goes through the following steps:

- Sizing, which adds starch, polyvinyl alcohol, or carboxymethlcellulose for strengthening.

- The addition of paraffin to smooth and lubricate the yarn.

- Mercerization, which involves dipping the yarn into a caustic soda solution and using acid to neutralize it. This process reduces fabric shrinkage, improves dye absorbency, and makes fabric feel smoother.

- Sometimes mordants containing lead are added to lock in the color.

- Woven cloth is dipped in a chemical finishing solution to improve the fabric's performance.[52]

Once the denim has been processed, it's sent to factories where it's cut into pattern pieces and stitched together, assembly-line style.

Finally, the trousers are sent to sites known as laundries, where they get their characteristic distressed look—scuffs, rips, fading, and all the other signs of a well-loved and well-worn pair of jeans. Distressed is an apt word for what happens at this stage because jeans are subjected to any number of harsh treatments. They might be scratched with sandpaper, blasted with diamond dust, soaked in enzymes, or drenched in formaldehyde. Or, they might be spattered with acid, bleached, put through mechanical abrasion, or splashed with potassium permanganate and other toxic chemicals.

Of course, chemical use isn't inherently bad, but when toxic substances are handled improperly or without proper protection, they jeopardize the environment and human lives. Many industrialized countries have environmental regulations, but in some places, these regulations are only weakly enforced, if at all. Take, for example, Xintang, China, which is known as the Jeans Capital of the World. In 2017, Xintang's three thousand jeans-related businesses had the capacity to produce 2.5 million pairs of blue jeans each day.[53] But the area has paid a high cost. The local rivers were stained dark blue, and the contamination became so severe that locals joked, "Xintang is so badly polluted that you can't give away houses for people to live there."[54] A 2010 Greenpeace report found the presence of five heavy metals (cadmium, chromium, mercury, lead, and copper) in the water and sediment. In one sample, cadmium exceeded China's national limits by 128 times.[55]

The majority of people willing to work in Xintang are migrants from other provinces, drawn by the allure of higher salaries. But once they arrive, the migrants find themselves in dire work conditions. One worker who wished to remain anonymous told Chinese journalists that most employees in Xintang don't have contracts or insurance and don't receive wages for the first three months.[56] Many of the migrants who live or work in close proximity to the denim plants in Xintang have reported persistent health problems, ranging from skin rashes to infertility.[57] Textile and dye workers are also at high risk for cancers, and today, the majority of these workers are women.[58]

After the conditions in Xintang became worldwide news, the Chinese government set out to curb the industry's environmental abuses. In 2018, they announced that they would open another Jeans Town in Changning, Hunan Province, where environmental concerns would take top billing.[59] But Xintang is far from the only place subject to the ravages of the blue jeans industry. Unsanitary conditions are unsettlingly common in places where labor is cheap and profit margins are razor thin, as is the case in many textile production facilities. All over the world, denim workers and their neighbors are subjected to unsanitary living conditions, all in the name of meeting the public's unstoppable hunger for cheap blue jeans.

You might wonder, "Why don't we just switch to organic jeans?" But I have bad news. Organic doesn't always mean sustainable, and producing organic cotton actually requires more resources.[60] Plus, even if the cotton were organic, the materials used to treat it probably wouldn't be. It's virtually impossible to buy a completely organic piece of clothing in today's mass market. Still, let's say the world came to a miraculous consensus and decided that we wanted to switch back to natural colorants. That wouldn't necessarily be better for the environment, especially if we wanted to maintain current levels of production. Recall that indigo is a land- and labor- intensive crop. With the annual worldwide consumption of synthetic indigo hovering somewhere around 50,000 tons, we would need to dedicate millions of acres of land to indigo in order to meet the current demand.[61] And that still doesn't account for all the water and other resources that farming so much indigo would take. Ironically, synthetic dyes might be just as eco-friendly as their natural counterparts.

Some environmentally conscious scientists have discovered a way to create a synthetic indigo that requires fewer chemical additives. The method relies on an engineered strain of *E. coli* bacteria, and researchers are confident that it can eventually be scaled up to meet production needs.[62] But Peter Hauser, a textile engineer and industry specialist, remains adamant that a new indigo can't solve our environmental problems. "[Bacteria-produced indigo] is not going to be any less polluting once it gets to the yarn," he explained.[63] Consumers simply love distressed jeans too much, and those are the processes that make jeans such an unsustainable product. As long as we want our blue jeans to look lived-in, they cannot be ecologically sound.

Blue Collar

It's hard to let go of that lived-in look because that's what makes blue jeans so special to begin with. Denim tells a story about the wearer. You can learn a lot about a person from the patches, wrinkles, worn spots, creases, and stains on their jeans. It's possible to identify the way they move and how they hold their bodies for the majority of the day. You can see what kind of work they do and where they've been. Miners' jeans, for example, usually have whiskering (the thin fade lines that come from repeated creasing) high on the waist, due to frequent crouching.[64] Even though jeans manufacturers artificially create these signs of wear-and-tear today, blue jeans' original popularity came from their status as hard-wearing garments for blue collar workers. Durability mattered more than fashion. That was something that Levi Strauss knew all too well.

On March 14, 1853, twenty-four year old Levi Strauss established a dry goods store in San Francisco. The young Jewish Bavarian immigrant had made his way west after realizing that he could make a fortune in the Gold Rush—not from gold, but from the miners themselves. At the time, San Francisco was an isolated outpost perched at the edge of the Pacific. Thousands of hopefuls flooded into its ports before launching themselves into taxing, rugged work.[65] With throngs of newcomers, limited supplies, and even more limited supply routes, Levi Strauss found a ready market. Miners easily wore their clothes bare, leaving them in constant search of heartier options like flannel, jean cloth, and duck cloth (which resembles canvas). Levi Strauss found success as a dry goods supplier and work-clothes wholesaler, but when his future business partner Jacob Davis approached him in 1872, he hadn't yet made any forays into clothing production.

Jacob Davis was a Jewish immigrant born in modern-day Latvia. He was working as a tailor in Nevada, using duck cloth and denim to make his wares, but in September 1870, he ran out of fabric. His relatives purchased some duck from Levi Strauss & Co. while on vacation in San Francisco, and pleased with the quality, Davis made Strauss his regular supplier.[66] In January 1871, one of Davis's clients ordered a pair of duck cloth trousers for her husband and asked Davis to make them as strong as possible. He decided to use the rivets he typically used for horse blankets to reinforce the sections that received the most strain.[67]

The idea was a rip-roaring success (or non-rip-roaring, as the case might be). Davis knew that he had come up with something special, but the cost of a patent was beyond his family's means. This wasn't Davis's first dalliance with being an inventor, and his wife Annie begged him not to pursue another fruitless endeavor. But Davis knew this time was different, and he decided to get some help. In July 1872, Davis reached out to his trusty cloth supplier, Mr. Levi Strauss. Davis explained that he was overwhelmed with orders for pants, and in fact, "found the demand so large that I cannot make them up fast enough." He revealed, "The secratt [sic] of them Pants is the Rivits that I put in those Pockets," and then made a bold proposition. If Levi Strauss would pay $68 take out a patent in Davis' name, Davis would give Strauss half the right to sell "all such Clothing Revited [sic] according to the Patent."[68] The negotiations proceeded apace, and on May 20, 1873, Davis and Strauss were awarded U.S. Patent

Number 139,121 for their process of making riveted work trousers.

Soon thereafter, Levi Strauss & Co. made their first riveted pants using 9-ounce XX blue denim (the strongest and heaviest type) sourced from the Amoskeag Mill in New Hampshire. The pants had one back pocket with the signature Levi's bow-shaped stitching, a watch pocket, a cinched waist, suspender buttons (no belt loops), and a rivet in the crotch.[69] These were the first blue jeans, although, I should point out that Levi Strauss never called them that—the company called their iconic trousers "waist overalls" well into the 1950s. The pants-style was also frequently referred to as "dungarees." Jean cloth was around for centuries, but the term "jeans" took a while to catch on. Its real heyday only occurred after 1950s teenage lingo went mainstream in the 60s.[70]

By the time the word "jeans" hit the scene, the garment had already become commonplace not only among miners and other physical laborers but also among the population at large. Within the span of a century, jeans went from a miner's dream to a closet staple. This wasn't an inevitable or even an expected journey. Only in hindsight does the popularity of blue jeans seem so natural. So, what pushed jeans firmly into the mainstream? To sum it up in three words: the Great Depression. Between 1929 and 1932, industrial unemployment in the United States hurtled from 1.5 to 15 million people.[71] Workers struggling to feed their families certainly weren't in the market to buy blue jeans. The same went for the farming families whose fields dried up during the Dust Bowl drought of the 1930s. Denim companies knew that if they wanted to stay in business, they had to find new customers—fast. One of the first places they turned was towards middle-class buyers.

Many middle-class Americans already had a romantic view of the American West, thanks to the popularity of Hollywood westerns. During the 1930s, epic characters like the Lone Ranger and Tonto intrigued radio listeners, while silver screen legends like Bob "Tex" Allen chased bad guys. Fascination with the Old West reached a fever pitch, and hundreds of dude ranches popped up all over the country, catering to tourists who craved rustic outdoor adventures. Soon, more than 25,000 families per year were visiting dude ranches in search of their own little slice of cowboy life.[72]

Denim companies happily jumped on the bandwagon and glorified denim-clad dudes in highly successful marketing campaigns. They created advertising focused on frontier themes, hoping to draw middle-class, urban-weary shoppers into their pool of buyers. Young boys wanted to look like Roy Rogers, and their city-slicker dads dreamed of riding horses and shooting outlaws. Denim companies also found a breakthrough market in women. In the early 1930s, celebrities like Katherine Hepburn, Greta Garbo, and Marlene Dietrich made a splash by wearing wide-legged dungarees, and other women wanted to follow the trend.[73] In 1934, Levi's launched Lady Levi's, and the following year, *Vogue* magazine featured the jeans as a must-have for any East Coast "dudines" headed west for a ranch vacation.[74]

Ironically, this vivid image of a denim-clad frontier life had been fabricated on the silver screen. Up until the 1920s, most real cowboys still preferred wool trousers. Even though jeans were durable, they didn't catch on quickly with cattle-rustlers, who considered denim to be the clothing of poor men and farmers.[75] Today, jeans are part of a cowhand's daily uniform, and many ranchers probably wouldn't suspect that Hollywood cultivated the idea of jeans as a cowboy garment. Nevertheless, by the end of the 30s, blue jeans and the American West seemed like natural partners, and they were forever welded together in the popular imagination.

Meanwhile, a burgeoning sense of worker solidarity created the largest swell of worker activism the United States had ever seen.[76] To use the evocative words of historian Donald Wooster, the ravages of the Great Depression and the Dust Bowl created "a generation of human tumbleweeds, cut loose from the soil." Between 1930 and 1940, approximately 3.5 million people moved out of the Plains states and migrated west in search of work.[77] Life, as most Americans had known it, had been upended, and in the midst of such upheaval, writers, artists, and singers set out to describe and trace the "real" America.[78] On the road, they found working people in overalls and straight-legged blue jeans.

In 1935, the state of California and the Federal Farm Security agency sent photographer Dorothea Lange and economist Paul Taylor to investigate the financial hardships the Great Depression had caused for farm workers. Lange's stark, dust-filled photographs depicted jean-clad drought refugees moving westward. These images of hard-working men and women in denim and cowboy hats, carrying their possessions along barren roads, echoed the popular myths of the Wild West. For the middle-class Americans unaffected by the droughts and dust, these people seemed like modern American pioneers, living lives of hope and hardship. Blue jeans, present in virtually every photograph and literary depiction of farm workers, became a quintessential part of that distinctive American tale.

In only a decade, blue jeans became a shorthand for the working class, the dream of the Old West, populist movements, egalitarianism, America's past, and its rugged, yet hopeful, present.[79] The infatuation only grew as time went on. Singing cowboys like Gene Autry appealed to Americans nostalgic for the pre-industrialized prairie, and as the number of actual ranchers and cowboys declined, the popularity of Western style grew.[80]

One of the most puzzling aspects of the history of blue jeans remains how a utilitarian garment became such a darling of high fashion. Luxury jeans retail at astronomical prices, but, materially speaking, there's no real difference between a $500 pair of jeans and a $50 one. Unless the jeans have precious stones attached, the cost difference goes entirely to marketing, advertising, buyers' overhead, or in rare (but laudable) cases, the factory workers' salaries.[81] It's equally puzzling that people will pay hundreds, if not thousands, of dollars for worn and distressed jeans. Most people would balk at the idea of buying scuffed sneakers or an unraveling sweater.

Yet these mysteries become less mysterious once one understands how blue jeans became popular in the first place. Many people today cling to the images that were cultivated in the 1930s. Culturally speaking, blue jeans represent a kind of crystallized longing for another era, another reality. In them, Americans see a connection to the past—to the idealized dreamscape of the West, preindustrial work, and adventure. Most people know that this idyll is fiction; a cowboy's work is a far cry from the sun-dappled dreams of a dude rancher, just as a miner's life is more darkness and danger than silver. Nevertheless, Americans like to blur the hard edges of the past. The earliest wearers of blue jeans were plagued by hunger, danger, and despair, but jeans no longer carry those connotations. Instead, they've become a sanitized symbol of the fighting spirit and resilient individualism of Americans.

Luxury denim taps into this cleaned-up image of the American past. A factory worker halfway across the world can spray jeans with potassium permanganate, so by the time they get to stores in Mexico, Minnesota, or Malaysia, shoppers don't have to do anything except open their wallets. They don't need to spend years roughing up the jeans or ripping them in all the right places. Purchasing a pair of distressed jeans is like buying a backstory, or at least the aesthetic of one. Distressed jeans bear all the signs of exertion, while the consumer never has to lift a finger. What could be more luxurious than that?

People today love pre-distressed denim for the same reason earlier generations loved singing cowboys. They're beautiful fictions that allow us to live in the most comfortable parts of our past without enduring the pain that truly went along with it. Blue jeans, like Westerns, cultivate a kind of nostalgia, a sepia-colored picture of the past. They're pleasant to live with and love, as long as no one digs too deeply beneath the surface.

2 CUT

All jeans are the same in the way that all people are the same, which is to say, hardly at all. We humans are cut from the same biological cloth, but when you start looking, we couldn't be more different. Male, female, Black, white, Asian, Hispanic, conservative, leftist, liberal, some of all, or none of the above. Jeans play the same elusive game. At first glance, every pair of jeans looks like cotton cloth stitched together to form trousers. But upon closer inspection, thousands of differences begin to appear—everything from fit and texture to color and stitching. Each pair of jeans is as unique as its wearer.

Perhaps that's why jeans have been so consistently and consciously used as a symbol of identity. They're a costume that immediately tells the audience who a person is. Am I a free-thinking rebel or a tight-laced conformist? Am I a hard-working cowboy or a street-smart fashionista? Am I a mother in ripped-knee jeans or a nonbinary teen in straight-leg denim? Over the course of the twentieth century, jeans have been used to perform identity, sexuality, and seduction—and they've done so with remarkable, almost unnoticed fluidity.

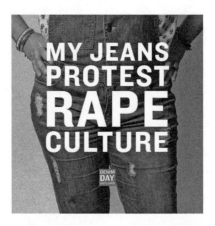

FIGURE 2.1 During the twentieth century, blue jeans became a political garment with a wide variety of conflicting meanings. This is an advertisement for Denim Day, a campaign designed to help eliminate sexual violence. Denim Day is a project of Peace Over Violence.

This fluidity has earned jeans the unique label of "superfashion." Blue jeans follow the changing tides of fashion while moving to their own seemingly timeless rhythm.[1] Even the most fashionable people may not succumb to the latest denim trends. Instead, they'll often opt for the style that they're most comfortable with or that they feel expresses their personality best. For example, in early 2021, a fleet of Gen Z TikTokers made fun of millennials' partiality towards skinny jeans.[2] Yet, only months later, a Cotton Incorporated survey revealed that forty percent of Gen Z gravitated toward skinny jeans, while the cool straight-leg crowd trailed with 38 percent.[3]

When it comes to jeans, shoppers don't always spend money to keep up with the times. Because blue jeans have this unique superfashion superpower, they're excellent indicators of personal preference. The style of jeans that a person chooses can reveal potent yet subtle details about who that person is and what they believe, value, and cherish.

The Wild One

At their inception, blue jeans were the go-to garment for people who made a living out of physical labor. Each piece of denim was saturated with the legacy of sweat and toil. It likely never occurred to Levi Strauss that his waist overalls would take off as a fashion statement. Yet, that's precisely what started to happen in the 1940s.

Beyond dude ranching circles and Hollywood blockbusters, blue jeans had earned the status of an outsider garment. On film, they looked glamorous, but in everyday life, they were also the attire of frontier toughs, prison-bound criminals, and Depression-era hobos.[4] Ironically, this outsider status helped push jeans firmly into the limelight of American culture. Youth looking to break free of rigid social norms draped themselves in denim as a proud declaration: *I'm counterculture, and I don't give a damn if you like it.* Supporters of the socialist movement adopted blue jeans as a sign of solidarity with the working class, and edgy undergraduates, intellectuals, and artists incorporated blue jeans into their wardrobe as well. The initial mass appeal of jeans had little to do with aesthetics, versatility, or style; the garment had cultural cachet precisely because it was anti-fashion. Young people across America were drawn to the casual cool of denim, and when their shocked parents responded with outrage, jeans only became that much more appealing.

In 1948, Levi's profits exceeded one million dollars for the first time, and the company made a conscious decision to move away from utilitarian advertising and focus on the creative vitality of the youth market.[5] In Levi's new marketing campaigns, jeans figured as carefree leisurewear, not the uniform of sweaty farmers or nine-to-five mechanics. Walter Haas, Jr., who eventually became the President and CEO of Levi Strauss, claimed that the shift was "inevitable," but at the time, changing the company's primary target market was risky.[6]

The risk paid off, and the demand for jeans continued to grow during the 1950s as stony celebrities with bedroom eyes and fitted jeans graced the silver screen. Robert Mitchum, Elvis Presley, Marlon Brando, and James Dean gave blue jeans a seductive bad-boy image. In *A Streetcar Named Desire* (1951), Brando sizzled in a tight T-shirt and equally form-fitting jeans. Despite the character's animalistic, immoral behavior, Brando managed to win the attention of American youth. Soon after, he cemented the iconic image of Levi's 501s in *The Wild One* (1953), a film about a group of unruly bikers. As the truculent leader of the Black Rebels' Motorcycle

Club, Brando gave young audiences a chance to vicariously experience a kind of rowdy joy, excess, and anger that most of them lacked in their daily lives.

Brando's films were part of a genre that came to be known as teensploitation. Troubled, oversexed, and disaffected youth populated movie screens with such regularity that once-shocking characters became commonplace plot devices. *Rebel Without a Cause* (1955) put James Dean's defiance front and center; *West Side Story* (1961) teems with teenage gangsters; *Untamed Youth* (1957) features two law-breaking sisters sentenced to farm labor; and *Dragstrip Riot* (1958) spotlights a competitive motorcycle gang that stirs up trouble with clean-cut youth. Through it all, jeans played a starring role. Even female stars like Marilyn Monroe and Doris Day wore cuffed jeans and cut up with denim-clad delinquents.

As the popularity of denim began to grow among teens, many American high schools banned blue jeans. Administrators associated the garments with low-class, rough-and-tumble behavior. But jeans brands had staked a great deal on the youth market, and they weren't eager to alienate parents who footed their children's clothing bills. In response, Levi's launched a fervent "Denim: Right for School" campaign featuring images of clean-cut, book-carrying boys in pressed jeans.[7] The ads didn't always work as intended, as one complaint letter from August 29, 1957 shows. An angry woman wrote to Levi's insisting, "While I have to admit that this may be 'right for school' in San Francisco, in the west, or in some rural areas I can assure you that it is in bad taste and 'not right for School' in the East and particularly New York . . . Let's not desecrate our schools nor promote juvenile delinquency."[8]

Disgruntled parents aside, it soon became clear that denim companies didn't have to worry. Adults weren't the only ones with pocketbooks, and blue jean companies made plenty of money from teenagers and twenty-somethings with disposable income and a penchant for rebellion. By the 1960s, jeans had become the symbol of youthful protest, and demand continued to rise. Peter Haas, another CEO and chairman of Levi's, recalled that in the 60s, "We kept putting plans together and exceeding them. There was no way to plan for the kind of growth we were experiencing."[9]

For teens growing up in the post-World War II period, jeans not only portrayed defiance, generational gaps, and economic disparities, but they also heralded strength in the face of an uncertain future. All those biker gangs, street toughs, and heroic loners weren't just rebelling against their parents. They were fighting back against the uncertainty and instability that the world had thrown their way. Wearing jeans became synonymous with refusing the status quo. Denim-clad youth embraced change, accepted the reality of violence, and refused to shy away from the darker aspects of humanity. While one might argue that youth culture was all about escaping into the fantasies of the silver screen, rock-and-roll, and fashion, there's a way in which youth culture was willing to face mayhem head-on. For many youth, challenging authority had become the new order of the day.

It took only a short leap from confronting authority to confronting oppression. By the early 1960s, the causes taken up by jeans-wearers had become larger than basic teenage angst. Young Black female civil rights activists tossed aside their "respectable" clothing in favor of jeans, denim skirts, and overalls. These young women wanted to embrace the clothing and cultural legacy of Black sharecroppers who had labored under an unjust system for generations.[10]

Jean-sporting female activists were radical, even within the context of the larger Civil Rights Movement. Many African-American leaders consciously used respectability as a political tool, and protestors sought to maintain their Christian morality in the face of unspeakable brutality. Civil rights activists faced attack dogs, water hoses, and savage beatings with dignity in an effort to take the higher ground and show that they were more "civilized" than their oppressors. Black women were especially tasked with the burden of proper comportment and dress. In the 1950s, an unprecedented number of charm schools cropped up, teaching Black women how to look and act respectable.[11]

Over time, though, many young women balked at these traditional roles, which they viewed as equally oppressive. They decided to use their appearance as a political tool. They stopped straightening their hair and opted for natural styles. They wore little or no makeup. And they slipped into the uniform of a working-class man: blue jeans. By adopting denim, these young women not only spoke out against racial injustice—they also sent a message to elders in the Black community who they felt blindly upheld Black middle-class gender norms.[12]

Imagine how striking it would have been when these women appeared en masse at demonstrations, community events, lunch-counter protests, and sit-ins. Blue jeans signaled their refusal of the racial, economic, and gender roles to which they were expected to adhere. Instead, these women chose to join the ranks of a larger 1960s-era youth rebellion, complete with its calls for equal rights, demands for personal and political autonomy, and newfound freedom of expression.[13] Jeans became a signature of personal liberation.

Around the same time but halfway across the globe, blue jeans were also playing a potent symbolic role for Soviet youth. In 1957, Moscow hosted the World Festival of Youth and Students, which kicked off the beginning of "jeans fever" in the USSR. In Soviet Russia, trousers had hidden pockets, so blue jeans—with their large and visible pockets—stood out. Wearing jeans became a clear indicator of an affinity for American culture and political values.[14] Journalists Alexéi Rudevich and Russkaya Semyorka recount, "Jeans were perceived not just as clothes but as a symbol of everything that was missing in the USSR, mainly freedom."[15]

For Soviet hardliners blue jeans became a symbol of excess, materialistic desire, and capitalism run rampant. Trade restrictions made it virtually impossible for Soviet youth to get their hands on an authentic pair of jeans, and if they did manage, they risked being expelled from university or fired. Worse punishments awaited those who dared to sell blue jeans on the black market. Today, the name of an American denim brand called Rokotov and Fainberg commemorates two Soviet men who were sentenced to death in 1961, partly for a charge of "trafficking in jeans."[16]

Still, the restrictions against blue jeans only seemed to make denim more desirable, and the black market trade continued apace. Eventually, the Soviet Ministry of Light Industry tried to make their own blue trousers, but jean-savvy citizens scoffed at the poor quality and fit. Similarly, in the German Democratic Republic, young people complained about the poorly made East German jeans knockoffs.[17] Youth behind the Iron Curtain wanted the real deal. They wanted jeans that faded in all the right ways, hung loose at the legs, boasted huge pockets, and announced to the world, "I'm a rebel." Blue jeans were such a potent symbol of freedom that in 1984 the French philosopher Régis Debray presciently remarked, "There is more power in rock music, videos, blue jeans, fast food, information networks, and television satellites than in all the Red Army."[18]

After the Berlin Wall fell on November 9, 1989, the fight for Western jeans drew to a close. American brands quickly swept into the untouched, jean-hungry market, and youth in former Soviet countries scraped together money to buy the trousers they had wanted for so many years. Blue jeans became more common, but in many parts of the former USSR, they retained much of their symbolic power. In 2005, jeans took on revolutionary significance once again during a popular uprising in Belarus. The president of Belarus,

Alexander Lukashenko had been in power since 1994, and he was widely known as Europe's last dictator because of his repressive policies. In September 2005, several months before an election, Democratic party supporters in Belarus took to the streets. Their leader had mysteriously disappeared, and many held Lukashenko responsible. During the protest, riot police confiscated the crowd's red and white party flags, hoping to steal the group's thunder. But one of the protestors, Nikita Sasim, removed the denim shirt he was wearing and waved it proudly, announcing that denim would be the protest's flag instead.[19]

It may have been a fluke that Sasim was wearing denim that day, but the blue flag struck an undeniable chord with the party's supporters. The series of conflicts that followed the September clash came to be known as the Jeans Revolution or Denim Revolution.[20] Celeste Wallander, an international relations adviser, explained to *ABC News*, "Jeans evoke the West. Denim is an assertive statement to show that [Belarusians] aren't isolated."[21]

During the build-up to the election, members of the youth movement Zubr wore jeans on the sixteenth of each month as part of a silent campaign for democracy.[22] Then, in March 2006, Lukashenko emerged victorious from Belarus' presidential election. Many were skeptical of the results, insisting that they had been fabricated, and thousands of protestors gathered in Minsk to dispute the election. For five days, people continued to gather, staying overnight in the freezing weather and braving the threat of riot police. Over their heads, traditional red and white flags waved alongside the newly symbolic blue ones.

The Jeans Revolution didn't succeed at overturning the election, but it was a formative moment for thousands of voters who have continued to organize. As of writing, Lukashenko still holds power, but the protests against him have become louder. In 2020, Lukashenko once again came under fire for the questionable results of Belarus' presidential elections, and thousands of Belarusians took to the streets to participate in the largest anti-government protests post-Soviet Belarus has seen to date.

Jeans continue to be a contested social and political symbol in other parts of the world as well. In March 2021, Tirath Singh Rawat, the chief minister of Uttarakhand, India, made a comment questioning the character of women who wear ripped jeans. After seeing a mother and NGO-head "showing bare knees, wearing ripped denim," he criticized Indian women's "run toward nudity." He continued, "If this kind of woman goes out in the society to meet people and solve their problems, what kind of message are we giving out to the society, to our kids?"[23]

Almost immediately, jeans formed the centerpiece of a protest, as members of the Delhi Congress women's wing took to the streets wearing ripped jeans, carrying children, and holding signs warning Rawat not to judge women by their clothes. On Twitter, influencers, actors, politicians, and other women used #rippedjeans to speak out against the minister's comments. In the immediate aftermath, Congress demanded either an apology or Rawat's resignation, while the minister doubled down. "I don't mind jeans," he replied, "but even today, I object to ripped jeans."[24] He informed the press that his real objection wasn't to naturally ripped jeans but instead to women who set a bad example for their children by cutting up new, costly jeans in order to fit the latest trends. (Rawat didn't mention buying new jeans with rips, but he likely disapproved of this behavior as well, since he took umbrage with women and youth "looking like rich kids."[25]) He insisted that a trend for patching jeans, instead, would teach children good values and discipline.[26] Several of his party members backed him up, saying that men and women need to wear "decent clothes."[27]

Rawat's claims reveal that despite how commonplace jeans have become, they still have the potential to be revolutionary. For Rawat, the material integrity of a garment supposedly reflects the integrity of its wearer; for his opponents, ripped jeans symbolize breaking free from traditional expectations, seeming relaxed in one's rebellion and defiant in one's comfort. The rip is precisely the point. And in the eyes of these mothers, their liberty sets a good example, not a bad one.

Hemmed In

No matter what you're into, chances are, there's a subculture to go with it. Like reading philosophy, drinking tea, and dressing like a 1940s Ivy League prep? The dark academia subculture might be for you. More into self-care, crystals, and wearing black? Try witchtok. Or perhaps baking bread, collecting trinkets, and putting doilies around the house sounds more like your speed. If so, there's a whole community of grandmacore lovers out there waiting for you.

Social media has not only brought like-minded people together with more ease, but it has also escalated the speed with which styles come and go. 2021 alone ushered in new style subcultures like dark academia, witchtok, grandmacore, cottagecore, and goblincore.[28] The social media platform TikTok is a self-proclaimed hotbed of cultures; that it hosts so much niche content has become one of its biggest selling points. The TikTok for Business website advises clients, "Subcultures are the new demographics."[29]

Today's world may be swimming in subcultures, but the term itself didn't gain traction until the 1940s.[30] At its most basic, a subculture is what its name implies: a culture within a culture. Yet, all subcultures share some unique features. For starters, every subculture is cohesive, meaning that the people who participate in it adhere to basic norms. Punks look like other punks, behave like other punks, and even think like other punks. Secondly, subcultures don't exist in total isolation. They define themselves in relation to culture at large by proclaiming, "We don't fit into *that*, so we've become a smaller community." As a result, most subcultures have some kind of oppositional element. They're reactive, at loggerheads with predominant social norms and expectations.

While many subcultures revolve around distinctive fashion choices, they can't be reduced purely to style. A person invests a more integral, more essential piece of themselves when they become part of a subculture. They make the subculture part of their identity and bring it into close contact with their deepest selves. I know this from personal experience, thanks to an adolescent punk phase. Much to my mother's chagrin, I wore plaid bondage pants, and my very nice prom dress was topped with a spike choker. But my choices weren't merely sartorial. They were a statement about myself—about the fact that I didn't fit into the norms of my rural East Texas high school, that I had a love of things I perceived as artsy and emotionally dark, and that I didn't care if other people at school knew it. This was a form of expression that set me apart from many of the people around me, but it also drew me closer to people who felt the same way. Subcultures are like a beacon in the dark that help like-minded people find each other.

Blue jeans may seem basic, but they've become an iconic linchpin of many subcultural wardrobes. In the 1970s, hippies broke free from restrictive, slim-fitting jeans, much in the way they broke free from the restrictive, slim-fitting social mores of their parents' generation. Bell-bottoms were both a political and social statement, often decorated with elaborate embroidery, appliqués, and paint as an expression of their unique wearer. There was also something androgynous about bell-bottoms, which fell into a perplexing nether region between maxi skirt and wide-leg trousers. Coupled with hippies' characteristic long hair, bell-bottom jeans drew attention to their wearer's anti-conservative, free-love, gender-blurring beliefs.[31]

In the 1980s, hardcore punks wore combat boots, torn jeans, leather jackets, and mohawks. Their clothing was a ripped assemblage of patches, paint, studs, and symbols, often resembling a craft project gone wrong. Frequently emblazoned with the anarchist symbol of a circled A, punk clothing took on an appropriately free-for-all aesthetic. Men wore tight, ripped jeans topped with a butt flap (a square piece of cloth that hangs over the backside like a reverse loincloth). Such jeans were a taunt, an in-your-face avowal of an "I don't give a fuck" attitude. Punk women sometimes adopted kilts, but blue jeans were still an important part of a female punk's uniform. Lauraine Leblanc, the author of *Pretty in Punk: Girls' Gender Resistance in a Boys' Subculture,* remembers how ashamed she was when her parents couldn't afford the latest "preppie cool" designer jeans. Instead of giving in to embarrassment, she made a style 180, shaved her head, and wore her old, ripped jeans with abandon. According to Leblanc, punk style gave her the strength to fight any criticisms thrown her way. "Yes, but at least *I'm* ugly on purpose," she told her tormenters.[32]

In the 1990s, sagging jeans became a controversial fashion choice, prevalent among young Black men, hip-hop fans, and so-called "wiggers," young white men who co-opted Black urban fashion.³³ Sagging allegedly began in prisons, where baggy uniforms were the norm. As a suicide prevention measure, prison regulations didn't allow belts, so inmates turned their ill-fitting trousers into a fashion statement. Soon, the fashion caught on outside of prison as a symbol of Black identity and freedom from oppressive, unjust systems. Sagging initially involved oversized jeans turned back to front, a style popularized in mainstream music by the duo Kriss Kross. Early sagging jeans dragged the ground and had a dramatically dropped crotch, which caused the wearer to adopt a swaggering gait. Over time, the jeans slimmed down, but the waistlines dropped even lower—typically, beneath the butt cheeks—so others could see the wearer's choice of designer boxers.³⁴

What started as a subcultural style quickly became a widespread controversy. Media exploded with articles lamenting the delinquency of youth culture and the supposed loss of morals. Public transit systems banned passengers with sagging jeans, schools suspended students who dared to drop their pants, and a number of states enacted public decency laws to punish the style.³⁵ Critics treated sagging like it was the fall of civilization as we knew it.

The style became such a hot-button issue because it was attached to Black youth. Leonard Jahad, a former law enforcement worker, now works as the Executive Director of the Connecticut Violence Intervention Program, an outreach program for at-risk youth. In 2014, Jahad pointed out that while other youth latched onto trends for baggy pants, "For [Black youth], law enforcement is looking at it like it's criminal."[36] He had a point. Consider how in the early 2000s many young women adopted a trend for whale tails (when the top of a thong peeks above the waistband). This daring fad caused moral panic and media controversy, as well as a hefty dose of slut-shaming, but whale tails were never treated as a criminal concern. There were no "Stop the Tail" billboards or "droopy drawers" laws passed against visible G-strings the way there were against Black youth's visible boxers.

Notably, it wasn't just white officials who spoke out against sagging. Black officials also approved of measures designed to curb the trend. According to the sociologist Michael Eric Dyson, this suggests that the controversy around sagging wasn't emblematic only of a racial gap; it also highlighted generational differences between Black youth and their elders. Dyson told the *New York Times* in 2007, "[African-American officials] have bought the myth that sagging pants represents an offensive lifestyle which leads to destructive behavior."[37] Yet, interviews with many of the saggers in question reveal that they never saw the style as a gateway to crime or an indicator of lawlessness. Instead, sagging jeans were a mode of shared expression that helped their community creatively unite, the same way other jean styles brought together earlier generations of artists, rebels, and activists.[38]

Sagging wasn't the only jeans trend in the 1990s to become associated with delinquent youth. JNCO jeans formed one of the most integral parts of street, skater, and self-identified "loser" teen style in the 1990s. JNCOs were hard to ignore. They were dramatic, hanging from the waist like an A-frame house before puddling on the floor. To call JNCOs wide-leg jeans is an understatement. Some pairs clocked in at an astounding 69 inches wide at the bottom.[39]

JNCO, which stands for Judge None, Choose One, was founded in 1985 by two Moroccan-born, French-raised brothers. The jeans were inspired by the wide-leg pants the duo saw as they walked around the Latino neighborhoods of East LA. The brothers decided to make a streetwear brand that would appeal to youth, and they commissioned a Latino graffiti artist, Joseph Montalvo, to design the brand's infamous crown logo. JNCO's motto was "challenge conventionalism," and within a decade, the brand had done just that. Their initial $200,000 investment jumped to a stunning $187 million in sales.[40]

Among teens, the jeans became a status of counterculture. Schools around the country banned JNCOs, which, as schools should have known by then, was a provocation to make kids want them more. A *Buzzfeed* article by Leonora Epstein broke down eleven reasons why JNCO jeans were so cool, but this one sums it up nicely: "Screw authority!" (Epstein also pointed out that the jeans made your legs into "monumental pillars of cool" and that "this was the only time in history in which girls could dress in mountains of fabric and still be considered sexy." As a historian, I'm skeptical of that second claim, but she's right that there was something transgressively hot about wearing forbidden, colossal pants.[41])

It's easy to wonder why people would get so irate about whether jeans have pockets, wide legs, or a fitted waistline. But those details hide a universe of assertions, accusations, and demands. For people within a subculture, a specific style of jeans can encapsulate an entire worldview. The tiniest features can announce political rebellion, a rejection of traditional beauty norms, an embrace of one's racial identity, solidarity with a disenfranchised community, or a challenge of conventionalism. Meanwhile, for people outside the subculture, those same details announce difference and defiance. A certain style of jeans can feel tantamount to a middle finger, an insult to the beliefs and ways of life they hold dear. Blue jeans are the perfect staple for two opposing groups: people who want to blend in and those who want to stand out.

It's All in the Jeans

In May 1943, the *Saturday Evening Post* had an unusual cover model: a woman with ginger curls perched atop a plinth. Her leather shoes rested carelessly atop a copy of Hitler's *Mein Kampf*, while she held a half-eaten sandwich. Her arm muscles bulged beneath the sleeves of her denim coveralls, and across her lap lay a mighty rivet gun. This was Norman Rockwell's version of Rosie the Riveter, WWII's now-famous feminist icon. The magazine sold millions of copies, and Rosie became a national treasure.

Although Rockwell popularized Rosie, he didn't create her. Rosie first appeared in a song by Redd Evans and John Jacob Loeb, which praised the women who joined the wartime effort. During WWII, millions of women flooded the U.S. workforce to compensate for the men who had gone off to war. For the first time, American women worked in lumber and steel mills, built dirigibles, joined assembly lines in munitions factories, unloaded freight, and sweated over heavy machinery. These were jobs that required not only a temporary relinquishment of traditional family roles but also a shift in traditional clothing norms. Women like Rosie wore dungarees, coveralls, and overalls just like their male counterparts had before the war. Jeans quickly became a beloved part of women's wardrobes.

But when the war ended, many Rosies lost their jobs, and the mythology of the perfect, apron-clad housewife took center stage. Women who had been riveters were now expected to exchange their jeans for feminine dresses and become riveting wives. Some women's magazines chastised readers for continuing to dress like mechanics, insisting that they resume their pre-war roles as full-time mothers and wives.[42] But once women had gotten a taste of blue jeans, it was hard to put that particular genie back in the bottle. Many women opted to wear jeans only in the most casual settings or at home, but others made denim a regular part of their public lives.

By the middle of the twentieth century, jeans had become a more gender-neutral garment. Today, women can wear baggy jeans just as readily as men can wear fitted ones, and in recent years, denim labels have fully embraced the idea of unisex jeans, explicitly targeting consumers interested in gender-neutral fashion. Levi's website specifies that their 501® Original has been gender-fluid for decades, and that fluidity "has never been more important than now, as our clothes become less about gender pronouns and more about unisex styles that work equally for all."[43] In the same way that jeans have blurred the lines between the working class and wealthy and between high- and low-fashion, they've also managed to blur the lines between male and female.

Nevertheless, jeans still have a complicated relationship to gender. On an obvious level, there are specific women's and men's cuts, but what's more fascinating is how the names for these cuts uphold gender norms. Take boyfriend cut jeans, which have a slouchy, relaxed fit. They conjure an image of a girl, smitten both with her boyfriend and his leisurely style. When she leaves his apartment, she shimmies into his oversized jeans and slips casually out the door. Jeans companies have managed to pack an entire narrative in two simple words—boyfriend cut—and with it, an entire bundle of gender- and heteronormative assumptions. A girl who wears boyfriend jeans doesn't simply wear loose jeans; she wears jeans that look like they were designed for men. But, the term "boyfriend cut" also carries a caveat. It says, "Wearing these jeans doesn't mean you have a real gender-bending need. It reveals a natural impulse to get closer to the object of your affection." In other words, "boyfriend cut" upholds traditional gender roles as much as it defies them.

Of course, there's a perfectly justifiable reason that the boyfriend cut got its name. Back in the 1950s and 60s when jeans were becoming popular in youth culture, it was fashionable for women to borrow their boyfriends' jeans (or their brothers', but I guess "brother jeans" just doesn't have the same ring).

Still, it's worthwhile to think about the terms we use for clothing styles. Because when we look hard enough, they reveal deep-seated cultural expectations. Consider mom jeans, which earned their name because every mom in the 1990s and 2000s owned a pair. These jeans have a relaxed fit and are extremely high-waisted, which has the bizarre side effect of making one's butt look long and flat. Mom jeans are practical, full coverage, and unflashy. They're the whole-wheat toast of the jeans world.

When the term "mom jeans" was popularized in 2003, it came with a stigma.[44] These jeans weren't motherly because they were somehow nurturing, calming, or reassuring. No, they were mom jeans because they were unflattering. Like what you'd see on a *mom*. Mom jeans and MILFs were, evidently, wholly incompatible.

This negative stereotype gained traction not because moms had somehow changed, but because youth culture had. Moms had worn high-waisted, relaxed jeans for decades with little trouble, but in the 90s, those jeans became a symbol of an out-of-touch, conservative way of dressing. Young women at the time tended to favor low-rise jeans, occasionally festooned with a whale tail. Pop culture icons like Britney Spears and Paris Hilton seemed to have a "how low can you go" competition with their jeans, and teenage girls replicated the limbo en masse, much to their parents' horror. These young women wanted to be alluring and liberated, like Gillian Anderson, who showed up to a red carpet event with her G-string showing. They wanted to be powerful, to own their sexuality and their bodies. They didn't want the perceived hum-drum lives of their mothers or the frumpy clothes that came with them.

Now those teens have come of age, and they've brought revised ideas of motherhood with them. A horde of hip mommy bloggers and Instagram mom influencers have rebranded motherhood completely. Women like Amber Fillerup Clark (@amberfillerup) and Heather Armstrong (@dooce) couldn't be further from the stereotypical image of the out-of-touch, flat-butt moms who were so brutally satirized by 90s and 00s media. This new crop of moms, some of whom were once whale-tailers themselves, has fostered a fresh take on motherhood. (Although I should stress that the mommy blogger image also frequently comes with flaws. Alpha-mom influencers insist that women can have it all: a pristine house, doting husband, perfectly behaved children, stellar career, camera-ready fashion, time for self-care, and perpetual self-confidence. Life behind the curtain is rarely so rosy, yet many mothers devotedly consume internet parenting content. Research shows that these mothers tend to see themselves as less effective parents.[45])

If being a mom no longer comes with the assumption that one has been put out to pasture, sexually speaking, the same goes for mom jeans. They may have loose, lanky backsides and a rumpled fly, but that doesn't make them any less hot. Many young women today actively want to wear mom jeans, with nary a care about the trend's effects on the collective topography of women's butts. In fact, they *like* the arguably unflattering style and loose fit that earned the jeans so much scorn. Mom jeans are comfortable, less gender-binary, relaxed—and they look perfect with the chunky boots and oversized tops that have also come back into style. Youth no longer see modest fashion as tacky, and many women lean toward comfortable, form-forgiving clothing. Fashion is sure to change again, as it always does, but at least for the moment, Zoomers have embraced mom jeans the way their grandmothers did, even if the context is different.

The same goes for dad jeans, which sit high on the waist and hang loose down the leg. Jerry Seinfeld and Steve Jobs wore dad jeans with total confidence, but by the time President Barack Obama took office, the jeans had already acquired their fatherly label and a healthy dose of contempt. Obama was raked over the coals in 2009 for wearing loose-fitting jeans to throw the first pitch at a Major League Baseball All-Star Game. Robin Givhan, writing for the *Washington Post* railed, "Few people want him to look like he spends his afternoons thumbing through his subscriber editions of *GQ*. But most folks would like to think he has at least heard the phrase 'dress for success.'"[46] Looking at the pictures now, the jeans look like the inoffensive straight-leg style that has once again become fashionable. Trendy retailers like Topshop and Rue21 even sell dad jeans for women. (In case you're wondering, they look like mom jeans with no tapering.)

The push for more inclusive, gender-neutral fashion is also changing jeans' sizing systems. Historically, women have been left to suffer under a vague, ever-shifting system of mismatched sizes. If someone is a size 10 in one brand, she may very well be an 8 or 12 in another. Online shopping reviews frequently advise whether certain garments run large, small, or true to size, but frankly, it seems like there's no truth when it comes to sizing.

Modern standardized sizing has its roots in the early 1940s. The US government commissioned a study of women's bodies in order to develop a standard labeling system for clothing, but the researchers quickly hit a wall when they discovered women didn't want to share their measurements with shopping clerks. As a result, the study concluded that women's clothing needed to follow an abstract metric that wouldn't reveal any specific body measurements, as with shoe sizes. In 1958, the National Institute of Standards and Technology issued the first set of even-numbered women's sizes (8-38). But within a matter of decades, the science-backed standard the government tried so hard to create had devolved into arcane hocus-pocus.[47]

While sizes serve a practical purpose—helping women find garments that fit—there are good reasons why standardization has failed. For even the most body-positive women, there's a deep, fragile psychology that goes along with sizing. Whenever a person doesn't fit into a ready-to-wear size, they immediately become aware that they have an "oddly" shaped body. Or when they wear a size 10 in one brand, they're loath to wear a size 12 in another. In the same way that earlier generations of women were reluctant to reveal their measurements to sales clerks, many women today feel reluctant to reveal how "plus" or "irregular" their sizes are.

Over time, standardized sizes encouraged greater attention to slenderness and the rise of "vanity sizing," or size inflation. Fashion brands have forgone their old, standard sizing systems, pushing toward smaller and smaller numbers in order to stroke customers' egos and turn a profit. Marilyn Monroe famously wore a US size 12, which would be equivalent to a US size 6 today.[48] Even though consumers hate the sizing madness, they still subconsciously gravitate toward clothing sizes designed to quiet their insecurities. Studies show that smaller sizes increase a shopper's self-esteem, making them more likely to buy the apparel in question.[49] That means brands have absolutely no incentive to make sizing less variable. Instead, they have every reason to try to cram shoppers into a single-digit spectrum. And we, the enablers, are perpetually at their mercy as sizing gets messier with each passing day.

Some garments, like tops or flowy dresses, are easier to size. But nothing will try a woman's patience more than trying to find a pair of jeans that fits. Research has shown that shopping for jeans creates more anxiety than shopping for virtually any other garment.[50] Viral videos show women comparing the "same" size of jeans from different retailers, revealing just how arbitrary those sizes are. I own three pairs of jeans, all of which fit, and each of which bears a different size on the tag. It's ironic that when it comes to shopping, the allegedly most comfortable garment is also the most nerve-wracking. Just the thought of carrying a pile of denim into a dressing room makes me feel fatigued and frustrated.

Some savvy brands have latched onto a simple idea—one they probably would have followed from the get-go, had measurement shyness not intruded: using basic waist and inseam measurements, as men's jeans do. For men, buying jeans is comparatively simple. Certain cuts fit differently, but if a man knows he's a size 36x32, he'll have a solid baseline to start with. (Still, men aren't immune to the vagaries of sizing; the journalist Abram Sauer discovered that many men's brands also cheat on their measurements to make their sizes more flattering.[51])

It seems that a sea-change is afoot, with more and more brands shifting to a measurement-based system. Many companies that cater to the under-forty set—like Madewell, Forever21, J. Crew, and ASOS—offer measurement-based sizing for women's jeans, and major denim brands like Levi's and Diesel have also opted for a measurement-based system. Some companies are experimenting with one-size-fits-all jeans in an attempt to reduce returned goods and wasted warehouse space, while others have turned to a custom-size business model, creating jeans specifically for individual buyers.[52] To be sure, cultural standards of beauty and body normativity will continue to be baked into the clothes we buy. As much as some may wish, the widespread preference for slenderness doesn't seem to be going anywhere anytime soon. But it does seem that jean manufacturers are gradually becoming aware that their customers are fed up with the abstruse numbering systems of the past.

The Denim Defense

What's the sexiest piece of clothing you can think of? I'm not talking about lingerie but about types of clothing you could see on the street. A nice suit? An A-line skirt? A freshly pressed button-down shirt? A low-cut blouse? If popular songs are to be believed, the answer is none of the above. In virtually every genre of music, from a wide range of eras, blue jeans have won the title of sexiest apparel.

In 1974, Jimmy Webb crooned about a charming denim-clad woman in "Lady Fits Her Blue Jeans," and in 1978, Neil Diamond gushed about a romantic night by the fire in "Forever in Blue Jeans." In 1984, David Bowie made the short film "Jazzin' for Blue Jean," which was all about chasing an irresistible girl. In the 1980s, country music joined the sexy blue jeans fray with Mel McDaniel's "Baby's Got Her Blue Jeans On" (1984) and Dolly Parton's "Why'd You Come in

Here Lookin' Like That" (1989). In 1996, seductive blue jeans hit the Eurodance scene with Sqeezer's "Blue Jeans," from the album *Drop Your Pants*. And since 2000, jeans have been all over the sexy hip-hop and R&B charts. See, for example, Ginuwine's "In Those Jeans" (2003), Chingy's "Dem Jeans" (2006), Flo Rida's "Low" (2007), and Chris Brown's "Blue Jeans" (2015). Pop and indie hits have also celebrated jeans' hotness: Katy Perry praised painted-on jeans in "Teenage Dream" (2010); Lana Del Rey professed her love to a James Dean-esque stud in "Blue Jeans" (2012); and the Kings of Leon revealed a fetish for a "Taper Jean Girl" (2014) on stages worldwide.

For decades, blue jeans have held the simultaneous title for the most basic piece of clothing and the sexiest. It may seem contradictory that a comfortable piece of everyday wear would also be the most tantalizing. But in almost every song in the Sexy Blue Jean Canon, comfort seems to be what makes jeans so erotic in the first place. A person confident and self-possessed enough to wear jeans on a date (or in a club or bar) doesn't need fancy clothes or elaborate makeup to send their lover around the bend. Their sex appeal isn't predicated on low-cut clothing or slick-tongued sophistication. It's natural. When a seductive person wears jeans, they can be seen as magnetic in their own right.

Of course, that's part of the allure that's been built around around jeans. They're easy, comfortable, and *real*. But if you've ever tried to squeeze into skinny jeans or tried to find a pair that didn't make your butt look too fat, too flat, or too anything else, you know that jeans aren't really that easy. Their ease is just as much an illusion as plucked eyebrows or a trimmed beard. All that natural ease takes work. Nothing conveys this paradox better than Calvin Klein's blue jean ads, beginning with a series of ads that were banned by the ABC and CBS television networks in 1980. Fifteen-year-old Brooke Shields teased the camera with a tight-fitting pair of jeans before revealing, "What gets between me and my Calvins? Nothing."

Shields' allusion to going commando wasn't the only thing that had networks up in arms. The ads took the power of suggestion to the level of a high art. In one ad, Shields struggles to pull on a pair of tight jeans while she explains that genes (and presumably jeans) are responsible for passing on a person's unique characteristics.[53] Her near-nude butt arches high in the air as she lifts her hips and wiggles into the jeans. She sprawls and writhes, twisting and turning on the floor in a tame yet allusive mimicry of sex. She fingers the top button on her blouse as she utters the words, "selective mating." She loosens her hair and stares forcefully at the camera—as brazenly confrontational as Manet's unclothed *Olympia* (1865). Then, she bends herself into a pretzel so her foot draws near to her face. Silhouetted against a white background, we see the supple curve of her inner thighs, the tight curl of her backside, and the triangular space left empty beneath her pelvis.

For most of the ad, Shields was fully clothed, yet there was little left to the imagination about either her figure or the ad's intent. This is the seductive power of jeans. Unlike most skirts, they offer full leg coverage while being more form-fitting. Unless the wearer also dons a longer tunic, the full line of each leg is clearly visible. This is why, in some parts of the world, wearing jeans with a shorter or more form-fitting blouse is still considered risqué. In a 2006 study of Mumbai youth and fashion, Shakuntala Banaji found that some young women like to use blue jeans' perceived sexiness to challenge gender expectations. One interview subject named Preeta told Banaji that she likes wearing "western" clothing "precisely because of what she saw as the transgressive, alluring, sexual, and 'come hither' associations."[54] For some young women, wearing blue jeans works like the Victorians' trope of the exposed ankle. Their bodies are completely covered, but the violation of cultural norms is taboo enough to titillate. Blue jeans are the modern, modest sign of sex appeal.

In some contexts, the sexual gaze inspired by jeans is welcome. Women like Preeta self-consciously use fashion to shape their identity and position themselves in relation to dominant cultural expectations. But in other contexts, that sexualized gaze is far less liberating. And it doesn't always require tight, obviously sexy clothing. In 1995, Calvin Klein's marketing team proved that even non-fitted jeans can seep with sex. In another banned ad, the English model Karen Ferrari appears with her back to the camera.[55] Her jeans are slouchy and low-slung. She's in a poorly lit room containing nothing but a paint-spattered work ladder. A male voice off camera says, "I like the way those jeans fit. Do you?" Ferrari spins around to face the camera as the male voice chides her for seeming bored.

"Can you dance?" the voice prompts.

"Yeah, I can dance. But I'm not going to dance for you." She looks uncomfortable as the man encourages her to entertain him. The camera zooms in on her hips and exposed midriff. It pans up across her chest. Ferrari rubs her face anxiously. Finally, she announces that she doesn't do things she doesn't want to do, and the male voice approves, "You've got a real good attitude," before the video cuts to the Calvin Klein logo.

Instead of feeling like commentary on independent women, the ad feels like a voyeuristic glimpse into the first thirty seconds of an unwilling sex tape. Viewers are invited, not to study the woman's jeans, but to study her body, her uncertainty, her discomfort. Moreover, they're prompted to find it alluring. The message of the ad shines through: a beautiful woman, even in a tank top and loose-fitting jeans, can be the subject of a sexualized gaze. In fact, the ad portrays her comfortable clothing as inviting. In their most casual moments, women often find themselves framed as willing sex objects, regardless of their intentions. And sometimes, as one Italian court found, wearing blue jeans even makes women sexually complicit.

On July 12, 1992, in the southern Italian town of Muro Lucano, forty-five-year-old Carmine Cristiano picked eighteen-year-old Rosa up for a driving lesson. After Rosa got into the car, Cristiano informed her that they had to pick up another student, and he drove the car to a remote location outside the city center. As Rosa later told the court, Cristiano parked in a small, empty street, threw her to the ground, removed her jeans from one of her legs, and raped her. Afterwards, he instructed her to drive back to her house and warned her not to tell anyone.[56] When she got home, Rosa's parents noticed that she was visibly upset, but she didn't tell them what happened. Several hours later, though, she cracked. The family reported the crime to the authorities, who called Cristiano in for questioning. He admitted to having sex with Rosa, but he told the police that everything had been consensual.

In February 1996, Cristiano was convicted of engaging in obscene acts in a public place, but he was acquitted of charges for carnal violence, private violence, abduction for the purpose of lust, and personal injury. Cristiano appealed his conviction, while the prosecutor appealed the series of acquittals.[57] In 1998, an intermediate appellate court found Cristiano guilty of all charges and sentenced him to thirty-four months in prison.

But the story wasn't over. Later that year, the Italian Supreme Court overturned the decision after finding that the appellate court had not evaluated the evidence thoroughly, "minimizing or ignoring . . . circumstances that were inconsistent with the alleged rape."[58] These circumstances included the fact that Rosa had waited several hours before telling her parents, the fact that she drove the car home, and what has come to be known derisively as the "jeans defense" to rape. The Court stated, "We must also consider that it is a fact of common experience that it is nearly impossible to remove jeans on another person without the wearer's active cooperation, after all [taking off jeans] is a difficult enough operation for the one wearing them."[59] In other words, because Rosa's jeans were too tight, she couldn't possibly have been raped. (Never mind the fact that no evidence appeared at trial regarding the fit of Rosa's jeans. Their tightness appears to have been speculation on the judges' part.)[60]

Public outrage quickly followed on the heels of the Cristiano decision. A group of female lawmakers showed up at Parliament wearing blue jeans and urged women across Italy to join their "skirt strike."[61] Alessandra Mussolini, a Parliament member and the granddaughter of Benito Mussolini, fumed, "The judges obviously have no sensitivity to the psychology of rape—no understanding of how victims think or how real life works."[62] Politicians and pundits across the political spectrum shared her viewpoint, including Simonetta Sotgiu, one of the Italian Supreme Court's ten female judges (out of 420 total). "The law is solidly in the hands of men," she lamented.[63]

In the United States, the protest caught the attention of Patti Occhiuzzo Giggans, the Executive Director of Peace Over Violence, a sexual, domestic, and youth violence prevention center headquartered in Los Angeles. Giggans came up with the idea of a creating a designated day for people to wear denim as a way of protesting the myths about why women and girls are raped. In April 1999, she organized the first Denim Day event and encouraged supporters to bring awareness to the cause, combat victim blaming, and educate others about sexual violence. Denim Day has become an annual event with millions of participants including elected officials, businesses, college students, and community members.[64] It takes place on the last Wednesday of April, which is Sexual Assault Awareness Month.

In the hands of the Italian Supreme Court, denim momentarily became a symbol of complicity. The Court's findings suggested that survivors of sexual abuse had renounced their right to consent simply by wearing blue jeans. But thanks to the Italian skirt strike and the ongoing work of Denim Day organizers, blue jeans have been reclaimed as a symbol of survivors' rights. While there is still a long way to go when it comes to preventing sexual violence and promoting sexual justice, the work of reformers around the world has had palpable results. Two years after the original Italian skirt strike, another accused Italian rapist tried the blue jeans defense. He claimed that intercourse with his ex-wife (the victim) had to have been consensual because she was wearing jeans. This time the Court admitted, "Jeans are certainly not a chastity belt and some models are easy to take off" before convicting the defendant.[65]

Thankfully, the denim defense was short-lived. And when it died, it took with it a dangerous, oppressive narrative: that blue jeans are an invitation to violate another person's rights. Blue jeans have long been "edgy" garments, steeped in the reckless refusal of social norms, defiance of gender expectations, and tireless mobilizing of activists who dream of a better world. But to this day, jeans have resisted any lasting cultural association with oppression. Across history, jeans have meant many things to many people, but time has shown a common thread: blue jeans always come back to their status as a symbol of freedom and hope.

3 COMFORT

It could be Paris. Or Dallas. Or Taipei. Every airport across the world looks roughly the same. Even in Shanghai, it's possible to find a Dunkin' Donuts when your jet lag kicks in. Yes, there are some architectural idiosyncrasies and signage in different languages, but all the major elements—seat arrangements, walkways, terminal layouts, and bathrooms—will seem familiar.

Such uniformity is intentional because airports function as "non-places." This term, coined by the anthropologist Marc Augé, refers to spaces designed to erase the specifics of history, culture, and identity. Sites like shopping malls, highways, and hotels facilitate global use, so that no matter who you are or where you're from, these places seem to make sense. By erasing cultural specificity, non-places promote easy circulation, consumption, and communication. A traveler arriving in a new city will have an instinctive sense of how to navigate the airport, collect their luggage, find a cab or take a train into a city center, pay the fare using a credit card, check into a hotel, and watch BBC News from the comfort of a king-size bed.

In our increasingly globalized world, non-places serve a powerful function. The more interconnected humans

FIGURE 3.1 Aside from the language and currency, this blue jean display would seem familiar to shoppers around the globe. Image courtesy of Getty Images, Burt Johnson, and EyeEm.

become and the more we depend on each other, the more ways we need to find to overcome distance and difference. Now, at the touch of a screen, we can contact people in the remotest parts of the globe. As Augé points out, today's telephones function as televisions, cameras, computers, and music players, meaning that people can "live rather oddly in an intellectual, musical, or visual environment that is wholly independent of [their] immediate physical surroundings."[1] Even our minds have become placeless.

But there are side effects to this ease. Because we have the world in the palms of our hands, we're no longer forced to confront the rich complexity of anthropological difference.

The human experience has, in some ways, been flattened. Efficiency and predictability take precedence over the element of messy surprise. While there may be minor inconveniences or slight discomfort, visiting a foreign country rarely entails truly disruptive experiences.[2] And no matter where you are in the world, you will likely share some frame of reference with the people who live there. When I visited the Sahara Desert, the guide and I chatted about a show he'd seen on MTV the night before. For better or worse, modern living has convinced humans to prioritize the global at the expense of the local.

If airports, supermarkets, malls, and roadways are the epitome of modern non-places, it seems fitting to consider jeans their sartorial equivalent. Over the last few decades, jeans have become a global garment, worn by all kinds of people in all kinds of contexts. Blue jeans are steeped in history, yet they masquerade as timeless, placeless, functional, and inconsequential. They're so commonplace that, for most people on the planet, putting on a pair of jeans barely even feels like a choice. Jeans have become the world's default attire.

Everywhere

In 1992, the Malaysian pop/hip-hop group KRU released their debut album *Canggih* (*Sophisticated*). Over the next two decades, the group went on to become one of the most iconic bands in Malaysian history, but their success was far from a forgone conclusion. While the majority of KRU's lyrics were in the Malay language, the band's songwriting and fashion sensibilities had a distinctly non-Malay cultural flavor that didn't sit well with conservative segments of the public. Objectors insisted that the band couldn't borrow so heavily from American hip-hop without losing their moral integrity. Eleven out of the twelve songs on *Canggih* were banned on government-owned radio for promoting "immoral western culture," and KRU's concerts were halted after several political leaders raised objections.[3]

Nevertheless, the band persevered, and by 1995 they had released their third full-length album, *Awas Da' Soundtrack* (*Watch Out Soundtrack*). On the song, "Negatif," KRU blasted the hypocrisy of critics who insisted they needed to draw on a single set of cultural references. As the band saw it, the problem was young versus old, not East versus West. They insisted that a desire to try, wear, and say new things doesn't signal moral corruption; it's simply a sign of changing times and preferences. The chorus demanded, "Leave me with my blue jeans."

To be fair to KRU's critics, when blue jeans first made their way to Asia, their in-your-face American-ness was a major selling point. In Japan, blue jeans were known as *jiipan*, or G.I. pants, because they were such an essential part of American soldiers' off-duty wardrobes. During the Occupation of Japan (1945-52), G.I.s frequently paid sex workers in old clothing. The women then sold the clothing to secondhand stores, which found a lucrative market in selling military surplus garments and American-style apparel.[4] In

Tokyo, one of the fastest ways to break from traditional norms and parental authority was to ditch one's school uniform and wear stylish American clothing. Youth who had seen denim-clad Hollywood stars slouch around onscreen yearned for the insouciant American style. Like their US counterparts, these young people quickly gained a reputation as delinquents, but that didn't stop them from buying blue jeans with abandon.[5]

By 1950, jiipan were so popular that retailers couldn't keep up with demand. Stores could sell a single pair of jeans at a 10x profit, often before the staff had a chance to put a price tag on it. Such high prices meant that only young actors, affluent artists, and rebellious teens from wealthy families could afford them. Jeans soon became a status symbol that connoted a curious mix of wealth and Western values. Even elites like the outspoken statesman Jirō Shirasu were photographed wearing Levi's. As Japanese fashion expert W. David Marx explains, blue jeans assumed a bipolar identity as a "an exclusive, rare garment simultaneously marred with the seedy connotation of black markets."[6] Jeans were the forbidden fruit, and sin was part of their allure.

Everywhere that blue jeans spread—America, Europe, Asia, and beyond—they entered the public eye with rebellious, transgressive bravado. But over time, jeans gradually became more commonplace. Once postwar manufacturing surged and global trade resumed, it became easier for denim-hungry youth to find the cuts they craved. As jeans became more available, they became more acceptable, and as they became more acceptable, they began to lose their American-ness. After the occupation ended, Japanese youth didn't have as many opportunities to encounter Americans or American culture firsthand, but they still flocked to blue jeans—not because they wanted to be American but because they wanted to be like their Japanese peers.[7] By the time blue jeans truly hit the mass market, they were no longer tied to American films, soldiers, or specialty boutiques. They were available everywhere, which meant they were just as Japanese as any other piece of clothing.

As similar developments took place in countries around the world, blue jeans lost their specific American resonance and earned their title as the world's most familiar clothing item. Today, many people see blue jeans as cultureless garments, even in areas where they are still worn only occasionally. In Kannur, India, only 5 percent of adults wear jeans in public. Yet, the anthropologist Daniel Miller discovered that most of the people he spoke with there assumed that jeans were an Indian garment. Only a small number of people associated blue jeans with the United States, and of those few, many had relatives living in the US.[8] In Kannur, the reluctance to wear jeans has nothing to do with resisting American culture— jeans had already lost their cultural specificity by the time they appeared in the region.

When KRU released "Negatif" in 1995, blue jeans were well on their way to becoming "non-garments" in Malaysia, but obviously they weren't all the way there yet. For the band's detractors, blue jeans were still a symbol of the decadent, immoral West, but for KRU and their peers, blue jeans were merely an expression of personal style. As far as young people were concerned, it was ludicrous to target denim as Western; blue jeans were just blue jeans.

KRU may not have been valorizing the West by wearing blue jeans, but the band was incorrect when they said there was nothing political about their clothing choices. If blue jeans really were a basic fashion choice—nothing more, nothing less—they wouldn't have been so symbolically powerful. But within the context of "Negatif," that single line about blue jeans carried a ton of symbolic weight. KRU didn't have to say, "Let me wear any non-Malay garments I like," or, "I have a right to wear whatever I want, regardless of whether it comes from the US, Europe, or anywhere else." All they had to do was insert "blue jeans," and the meaning became clear. Jeans had become the perfect symbol for open-mindedness and placelessness. When the band told conservative Malaysians to stop worrying about jeans, they were really saying, "Stop policing my personal choices. We're living in a global world now." Jeans were no longer the emblem of American values; they were the emblem of a larger, worldwide culture.

As humans across the globe have become more economically interconnected, we have also become more culturally interconnected, and blue jeans are one of the tightest threads that bind us together. No other garment is as universally popular. Jeans have made inroads into the most isolated corners of the world and have found popularity among people of all races, faiths, and genders. They're the garment that refuses to be stopped. Every year, blue jean sales grow by leaps and bounds. Between 2013 and 2018, the world market for jeans grew 8.9 percent, with the fastest growth in Latin America, Asia, and Africa.[9] In Mexico, 98 percent of consumers own at least one pair of jeans, and nearly one in four people say that they wear jeans every day of the week.[10] In China, jeans spending has been projected to rise 14 percent by 2024 to reach a whopping $13.4 billion. (Compared to the 4 percent growth anticipated in the U.S. market, that's a huge increase.[11])

The popularity of blue jeans is even on the rise in countries that have previously tended to steer clear of them. India has the lowest jeans adoption rate worldwide, but in a 2021 survey, more than 40 percent of Indians stated that they "love" or "enjoy" wearing denim.[12] Even in Kannur, the city where only 5 percent of adults wear jeans in public, the percentage of people who wear jeans in private is higher. For example, almost all unmarried teenage girls in Kannur admitted to owning jeans but said they only wear them while traveling.[13] Jeans have also made their way into Indian pop culture and entertainment. In Bollywood films, heroes and heroines wear jeans with such regularity that one costume assistant reported, "I cannot think of a film where we haven't used jeans, even [on] actresses."[14]

Jeans have been seamlessly integrated into so many countries thanks to the growth of industrial global capitalism. Mass production has not only lowered the manufacturing costs of blue jeans, making them affordable at all price points, but it has also raised their visibility as a worthy garment. One of the world's largest denim plants, Arvind, is headquartered in Ahmedabad, India. The company produces textiles for worldwide brands like Lee, Tommy Hilfiger, Calvin Klein, and Gap, and their extensive marketing and partnerships have helped make jeans more visible within the Indian market as well as other markets worldwide.

Arvind employs more than 30,000 people within India and plans to expand their domestic workforce further.[15] When a person's livelihood comes from manufacturing a single garment, it doesn't take a leap of the imagination to realize that soon, that person might start wearing the garment. Especially when it's a garment known for being cheap, durable, and suitable for hard work. Their families and friends might also adopt the garment, and before long, the garment becomes normalized.

Arvind is a blue jeans juggernaut, but it's certainly not the only company whose bills are paid by denim. Other companies such as the Taiwanese clothing manufacturer Roo Hsing run facilities in locations across the globe. Mexico, Cambodia, Myanmar, Tanzania, Bangladesh, Nicaragua, Pakistan, Brazil, and China have all become major centers of blue jean production. The more global the scale of production becomes, the more global the product itself becomes. The mega-industry of denim is a beautifully oiled self-propelling machine.

Everywhen

Walk into almost any clothing store that sells jeans, and you'll be faced with an overwhelming set of choices. Do you want straight-leg, skinny, curvy, wide-leg, demi-boot, or flare? The finishes are equally varied, and specific styles conjure potent memories of specific historical eras. Looking at a pair of acid-wash jeans conjures the 80s the same way the fluted curves of bell-bottoms recall a summer full of free love and hippies. Yet, somehow, blue jeans magically seem to defy the endless parade of seasons. Fashion magazines and popular culture reinforce the idea that jeans are a staple that will never go out of style. Designers maintain that a good pair of jeans is an investment piece that will last a lifetime, presumably justifying an elevated price. The words "classic" and "blue jeans" go together almost as well as the words "classic" and "Coca-Cola."

What makes jeans' perceived timelessness especially ironic is the ever-quickening pace of denim trends. Depending on who you ask, the most stylish jeans right now might be slim leg, skinny leg, wide-leg, baggy, fitted, high-waisted, or low-slung. What one fashion publication deems out, another deems in. Options are seemingly endless, and the most defining trend of recent years seems to be the lack of a dominant trend at all. As Haley Nahman pointed out in the *New York Times*, "These days, new styles emerge and recycle at dizzying speed. So fast, in fact, that sometimes they seem not to move at all, like a colorful spinning wheel transformed into a blur of brown: everything relevant at the same time."[16] The trend cycle has become so compressed that it's virtually non-existent.

Maybe that's why jeans seem so timeless. If everything is trendy, nothing is out of date. We've resurrected styles from the 70s, 80s, 90s, and 00s all at the same time, condensing decades of fashion into a single moment. Jean styles are no longer attached to a specific era; they're part of the endless mish-mash of capitalist production gone wild. When we look back thirty years from now, it's likely that the defining characteristic of today's fashion will be its sheer variety and abundance, not a particular look.

Consumers no longer base their choices solely on what they see in fashion magazines or their local mall. They go fishing in the vast fashion sea of the internet. Targeted advertisements segment consumers into hyper-specific niches, influencers can change the direction of fashion in a matter of seconds, and clothing retailers offer more options than ever before. As of writing, a quick search for "jeans" on the clothing website ASOS turns up more than 6,200 results. If you can dream a piece of denim, you can probably find it.

This shift away from dominant trends has been hailed as the rise of "personal style," which allegedly offers consumers new possibilities for self-expression and individuality.[17] But as Nahman's article reveals, personal style might not be all it's cracked up to be. If fashion trends often express shared meanings or values, what does such a highly individualistic take on fashion say about the world today? Have we become more atomistic, more focused on ourselves than the collective? Have we bought into the idea that mass production and industry hold the key to self-expression? Have we decided that the "more is more" ethos is worth the personal benefits, even at the cost of the environment?[18] The answers to these questions may not be simple yeses or noes, but the historian Niall Ferguson was onto something when he stated, "That mass consumerism with all the standardization it implied could be reconciled with rampant individualism was one of the smartest tricks ever pulled by Western civilization."[19]

"Trick" might be just the right word for blue jeans' perceived timelessness. Like a trick of the light or a magic trick that works by misdirection, blue jeans have managed to convince us that they're perennial. It's as if they've always been there and always will be. Yet, as we've seen, blue jeans aren't old, historically speaking. They were invented around the same time as the earliest automobiles, but they only entered the cultural primetime half a century later, well after vacuum cleaners and automated washing machines had taken American homes by storm. Still, within a handful of decades, they had become such an indispensable part of global fashion that it's difficult to remember a time before they were part of our wardrobes.

If anything, this is a testimony to how short our collective memory can be. Many of the things people take for granted as timeless inventions are, in the grand scheme of things, surprisingly new. When an object becomes entrenched in daily life, it quickly loses its history and takes on an air of permanence. The more frequently we use a given object, the more familiar it becomes—so familiar that it seems as if it's always been there. Just as it's difficult to imagine life without a smartphone (even though I've spent more than half of my life without one), it's difficult to imagine a world without blue jeans.

I suspect that this enduring quality is, in part, a function of the material itself. Denim and jeans have been conflated to the point that they're almost synonymous, and denim was built to last. It was created to withstand hundreds of washes, conforming more and more to the body as time passed. It could handle dirt, tools, grease, brambles, and cattle. Denim is a thick, hard-wearing fabric, designed to be practically eternal. Indestructible. Immortal. It's the sartorial equivalent of a vampire. Perhaps that's why, even after jeans became a common part of leisure wear, they maintained a reputation for being long-lasting. Whether a person purchased straight legs or boot cuts, the result was the same—those jeans would last because they were made of denim. Even if the cut wasn't enduring, the object itself would be.

Still, given the proliferation of options today, one must consider what defines a pair of jeans in the first place. Denim fabric was one of blue jeans' early defining characteristics, but the rise of synthetic fibers like polyester, elastane, and lycra have permanently changed the landscape of jeans-buying. Consumers, particularly in America, have shown a marked preference for stretchy jeans. Jeans made with raw denim have a breaking-in period, but many customers want the instant satisfaction of comfort. When super-stretchy jeggings hit the market for the first time in 2009, sales skyrocketed. And between 2011 and 2017, the percent of stretch denim jeans in the U.S. rose from 44 to 75 percent.[20] Globally, shoppers still prefer jeans made with cotton, but raw denim has ceased to be a mandatory component of jeans.[21]

If pure cotton twill isn't a timeless component of blue jeans, then what about their iconic color? The word blue is in the name, after all. Yet, jeans today run a whole gamut of colors and patterns. White, black, caramel, and olive comprise the more neutral options, but even the most iconic brands offer jeans in every color of the rainbow. Zebra-stripe jeans, checked jeans, high-waisted dinosaur-print jeans? All can be found with a simple Google search. Blue may still be the most iconic color for jeans, but it's not an essential feature.

If we're sticking to an originalist interpretation of the term "blue jeans"—with their heavy cotton cloth and indigo-blue dye—true blue jeans have been outnumbered by the thousands of alternative options on the market. So, what is it that makes jeans *jeans*? One might think that meeting only one of those criteria is enough. A pair of black denim trousers would qualify, as would a blue pair made with a polyester blend. But a quick trawl of shopping websites reveals that the term is far more flexible. A pair of pleated lilac corduroy trousers masquerades as "ultra wide-leg jeans," translucent polyurethane "jeans" bare the wearer's most intimate secrets, and men's rubber "jeans" with lace-up sides are, evidently, a thing.[22] Strictly speaking, jeans don't even have to be pants, given the wide range of options without legs, a backside, or crotch.

Most people seem to have an intuitive sense of what "jeans" refers to, and the world of fashion hasn't devolved into chaos because of the myriad variations. But that's what's so fascinating about blue jeans. The term has expanded to accommodate an entire universe of apparel, including garments that don't have any of jeans' original defining features. This suggests that the cultural attachment to blue jeans isn't so much to the historical garment as to the general idea of jeans: a casual, comfortable piece of clothing that adapts to the wearer's needs. Perhaps that's what truly makes jeans timeless. Individual styles may evolve, but the category as a whole—and what it represents—is here to stay.

Everyday

There are rare moments when wearing jeans can make a splash. In 2001, Britney Spears and Justin Timberlake wore head-to-toe denim to the American Music Awards, an event that typically requires formalwear. They made waves for their brazen defiance—so many waves, in fact, that, twenty years later, Justin Timberlake begged the internet to forget about his moment in the chambray spotlight.[23] But most people don't have the opportunity to walk a red carpet, much less to fly in the face of said carpet's conventions. In daily life, wearing denim rarely draws excessive attention.

Instead, people sometimes stand out for *not* wearing denim. Blue jeans have become so commonplace that forgoing them can, at times, seem like a radical act.

Throughout my twenties, I favored dresses over jeans, and I was surprised by how often I was asked, "Why are you so dressed up?" Eventually, I bought a pair of jeans, and almost immediately, I stopped receiving comments about how I dressed. I hadn't made a conscious choice to fit in, but in retrospect, the slight touch of anonymity felt good.

Blue jeans occupy a permanent role in our closets as much for what they *don't* say about us as for what they do. When you want to get on with your day and move about unnoticed, jeans are a reliable go-to. Such ease and uniformity are precious in the modern world. Life moves at such a disorienting pace that business theorists have even come up with a tidy acronym to describe its whirlwind character: VUCA, or volatility, uncertainty, complexity, and ambiguity. In such frenetic conditions, humans need tools to maintain routine and stability. Within global architecture, non-places provide predictable, steady interactions. A car will always go between the lines in a parking lot. A hospital will always have some form of urgent care center. An airplane will always take off from a clearly designated gate. In the world of apparel, blue jeans serve that same orienting purpose. As fast fashion throws every imaginable combination of colors, cuts, and styles at consumers, blue jeans remain the "non-garment" in the closet. They orient and unify us, even as the world moves at a lightning pace.

The philosopher and sociologist Georg Simmel (1858-1918) was not alive to see blue jeans' ascendancy, but he astutely predicted the role they would play in the wardrobes of modern consumers. "Fashion is only concerned with change," Simmel explained, yet there are a few garments that manage to rise above the never-ending cycle of change. These so-called "classic" pieces "possess an air of composure, which [resists] modification, disturbance, destruction of the equilibrium."[24] In Simmel's estimation, classic objects (like blue jeans) serve as the eye in the center of the sartorial hurricane. They're a still point—a garment everyone can agree on and wear with certainty. Jeans can be dressed up or dressed down. They can be worn at home, at church, or in fancy restaurants. They can even be worn to captivate the world, as Steve Jobs demonstrated when he donned jeans to announce the invention of the iPod, iPhone, and iPad.

In some ways, blue jeans have come full circle. A garment that began as nondescript workwear passes, yet again, for nondescript workwear—even in environments that used to be the exclusive domains of suits and skirts. In the 1950s, Hewlett-Packard began experimenting with relaxed Friday get-togethers known as Blue Sky Days. Employees could dress casually, use their time to discuss new ideas, and end the day with a beer bust.[25] Other scattered instances of what later came to be known as Casual Friday slowly began to pop up as well. In 1962, Hawaii's state Fashion Guild instituted Operation Liberation, a campaign to make the traditional Hawaiian shirt a standard component of business attire. A few years later, Aloha Friday became a weekly event in Hawaiian workplaces.[26]

Still, the concept of Casual Friday didn't catch on across the US until the 1990s, when businesses wanted to raise company morale without boosting paychecks. Once workers had the opportunity to ditch their suits and ties, a new clothing industry sprang into life: business casual. Levi's savvily expanded their Dockers brand by making khaki trousers a signature "biz-cas" look, but they also suggested, "Jeans can be paired with a blazer or sweater."[27] Now, 50 percent of U.S. companies allow workers to dress casually every day, and 62 percent of consumers report wearing denim to work at least three times a week.[28]

In large part, blue jeans have become so desirable because they're comfortable. Whether they're destined for work, home, or a night on the town, blue jeans allow the body to move freely. Because denim has a breathable weave, jeans trap less heat than dress pants, and cotton twill grows softer over time. Jeans also hide stains well, making them perfect for a quick lunch on the go. Of course, jeans aren't as comfortable as sweatpants or leggings, but with stretch denim factored into the equation, they can come close, without slipping into pajama or workout territory. Jeans walk a fine line between comfort and class.

It may seem natural that people gravitate toward more comfortable clothing, but comfort hasn't always been among consumers' chief concerns. Before the modern era, people often placed other values like utility, multifunctionality, and display over today's familiar values of ease and intimacy. Many a grandiose home featured opulent four-poster beds with lumpy straw mattresses and magnificent dining tables with unyielding, Puritanical seats. These objects were beautiful to look at, but they left a lot to be desired in the coziness department.

In Europe and America, the eighteenth century ushered in a new "age of comfort." The upper classes rejected the rigid furniture that had been designed to showcase their stately posture and instead favored new furnishings, like cushioned armchairs and sofas. Wealthy homeowners began to create function-specific rooms with full privacy, like bathing rooms, nap rooms, and social rooms (small spaces designed for relaxation with one's closest friends).[29] Upper-class fashion took a decidedly breezy turn, causing the French king Louis XIV's sister-in-law to complain of palace visitors, "It was as if they were dressed for bed."[30] Smaller comforts also found their way into the middle and lower classes. Soft cotton garments were more liberating than scratchy wool or coarse linen, and heating accessories like warming pans and braziers became popular among even the most hardened peasants.[31]

With the rise of global capitalism, shoppers were tantalized by a variety of comforts, all promising to ease the aches of life. New furniture promised to relieve tired feet. New clothing promised to free the body. New trinkets and doodads promised to provide more wonder, free time, and delight. Mass production and industrialization often exacerbated the plight of the working classes, but these same processes also made it possible for them to afford small niceties. Comfort became a deeply entrenched cultural value, regardless of one's social status.

The architect Witold Rybczynski has argued that since the eighteenth century, "Comfort has changed not only qualitatively, but also quantitatively—it has become a mass commodity."[32] The longing for comfort went into hyperdrive as more and more products emerged, claiming to make people's lives easier. During the twentieth century, technology revolutionized homes, workplaces, and businesses, bringing new kinds of convenience and ease. Microwaves. Air conditioners. Refrigerators. Running water and electricity, even in remote areas. Automobiles. Computers. Smartphones. Name virtually any convenience, and it was probably fine-tuned for comfort during the last century.

With so many conveniences at their fingertips, people refused to settle for things that simply looked good. They also wanted to *feel* good, and with that came an increased love of casual living. Gone were the days of hoop skirts and fussy cravats. Women abandoned corsets for less restrictive undergarments, and men eventually lost interest in vests and three-piece suits. Fashion historian Deirdre Clemente observed that the relatively recent rise of casual style has undermined fashion rules that existed for millennia. For much of recorded history, the rich literally wore their social class on their sleeve through conspicuous consumption. The wealthier the person, the more luxurious the fabric, colors, and craftwork that went into their clothes.[33] Now, moguls and millionaires don hoodies and sneakers, and people climbing the corporate ladder have become more vocal about their preference for a relaxed dress code.

During the transition from a formal business culture to a more casual one, blue jeans were perfectly positioned to become the new Relaxed Garment in Chief. They could still be tailored to fit, giving the wearer a polished look that announced, "I'm so comfortable in my own skin, I don't need a suit to make me look authoritative." In 2009, the *Wall Street Journal* heralded "the relentless rise of power jeans," which they spotted on world leaders in increasing numbers.[34] Today, it's no surprise to see jeans on the most prominent executives. Mark Zuckerberg wears a daily uniform consisting of a gray T-shirt and jeans. Likewise, Google CEO Sundar Pichai and Microsoft CEO Satya Nadella appear frequently in slim, stylish jeans. No one questions the professionalism or talent of these individuals (at least, not for their decision to wear jeans). If anything, observers frequently praise Silicon Valley CEOs for their sartorial practicality, simplicity, and confidence.

The trend toward casual living isn't unique to the United States. In 2014, the fashion writer Muireann Carey-Campbell lamented over how Americans' "casual approach to dressing has gone global."[35] Streetwear, sportswear, and athleisure have flooded stores worldwide, facilitated by the extensive tendrils of global capitalism. Youth in Japan can buy trendy flannels and selvedge denim from the Harajuku label NEIGHBORHOOD, while stylish Brazilians can buy denim from Tufi Duek, founder of the brands Triton and Forum. The desire for casual comfort—with denim at the helm—has spread across the globe.

Perhaps blue jeans have so successfully become an international "non-garment" because, like non-places, they satisfy a collective need for ease. But, one might wonder, why has this deep longing for comfort taken such firm hold in the first place? Comfort has obvious physical appeal; there's nothing quite like the hug of a familiar pair of jeans. But the craving also runs deeper. Comfort has profound psychological effects. It generates a feeling of security, safety, and stability. The rest of the world may be a fast-paced mess, but when a person is comfortable, they have access to an underlying sense of tranquility. The more at ease a person feels, the more easily they'll be able to navigate the stresses and challenges of life.

Wearing blue jeans also allows people to bypass a great deal of anxiety—anxiety about standing out, fitting in, wearing the right thing, looking the right way, giving the right impression. Thanks to jeans, people can move through life with less worry. Is it any wonder that so many people want to wear them every day?

Everyone

In *The Story of Doctor Dolittle* (1920), the world's most famous veterinarian discovers a fantastical creature called the pushmi-pullyu. This gazelle-unicorn hybrid had a head on each end, making it the physical embodiment of a game of tug-of-war. When one head led, the other necessarily followed, and vice versa.

I was reminded of the pushmi-pullyu the first time I read Georg Simmel's description of fashion as a constant push and pull between opposing forces. On the one hand, fashion creates the perfect opportunity for individual expression. A person's pushmi fashion spirit can inspire them to crave bright colors, outlandish cuts, or unusual combinations. They might want to free themselves from gender norms or the dictates of "good taste," expressing their innermost desires through their outermost apparel. But as soon as the pushmi forges ahead, it gets jerked back by the second, pullyu head: social convention. Fashion demands uniformity, especially among one's economic class or people of the same ideological persuasion. We dress like the people around us or those we aspire to be like—either out of sincere admiration or fear of embarrassment.

Imitation is a fundamental component of human development, Simmel points out, and it encourages like-minded humans to band together.[36] Few garments are more unifying than blue jeans. No matter who you are, what you believe, where you live, or where you come from, there is probably a pair of blue jeans in your closet. That's what makes them so appealing to designers like the South African creator Tshepo Mohlala, who has boldly declared, "Denim has no race. It's a fabric that can unify the world."[37]

Even though jeans have now reached Simmel's rare "classic" status, the pushmi-pullyu dynamic is still very much in effect. Take, for example, Versace's thigh-high denim boots from the 2019 Pre-Spring collection. Each stiletto boot resembled a miniature pair of jeans, complete with belt loops, pockets, and a leather belt. The boots slouched over the calves, making the wearer look as if they had pulled their jeans down in the restroom and neglected to pull them back up. Few would have expected these thousand-dollar caprices to appeal to the masses, but when fashion-forward celebrities like Jennifer Lopez donned the boots, the pullyu of social imitation surged forward. The great unification began, and retailers like Forever 21 created their own versions that sold at a more modest price in the double-digits. Soon, aspirational fashionistas everywhere could flaunt their own mini-jean boots.

Sometimes the dynamic works differently, with elite brands and mega-retailers copying society's DIY renegades. This was the tug-of-war that fascinated the anthropologist Dick Hebdige, who set out to explain why the styles of so many anti-fashion youth culture movements—like punks, mods, skinheads, beats, and teddy boys—had lost their edge. In the 70s, mohawks, ripped pants, safety pins, and patches popped up on English youth, bringing with them a devil-may-care attitude. Traditionalists clutched their pearls, and frustrated parents bemoaned their children's hard-edged malcontent.

Initially, these deviant subcultures garnered media attention because of their adherents' transgressive attitudes and anti-social behavior. But the more often anarchic icons like Sid Vicious appeared in the public eye, the more the public became accustomed to them, identified with them, and, in some cases, idealized them. Apparel brands latched onto the most marketable elements of punk and began to churn out punk-influenced styles. Record labels signed more punk bands. And soon, punk had moved from the bedrooms and garages of youth into the marketing departments of corporations. It took only a few years for punk's once-defiant fashion statements to become co-opted and commercialized by high-street retailers and high-end fashion magazines.

According to Hebdige, this cycle of appropriation wasn't an anomaly; it was an inherent feature of capitalism. Think of it this way: mainstream culture and consumerism go hand-in-hand. The more people chase trends, popular media, fashionable clothes, and current ways of thinking, the more stuff they're inclined to buy. This is true even of minimalists; look at how Marie Kondo's life-changing magic flooded bookshelves or visit any Container Store to find an organizational smorgasbord promising a more streamlined life.

Subcultures aren't immune to consumerism, but they do tend to emerge in opposition to the mainstream. The first punks didn't buy loincloths and shredded denim from a store; they used the materials they had at hand. Garbage bags, safety pins, pillowcases—no household items were safe from a punk's grasp. This DIY spirit suits subcultures because, as Hebdige explains, the point of these groups is to express "a fundamental tension between those in power and those condemned to subordinate positions and second-class lives."[38] A subculture's style isn't only about looking cool. It also serves an ideological purpose, compensating for a lack of social power. People who don't fit into the mainstream can come together through fashion to make themselves heard.

Unfortunately, subcultures rarely have the chance to stick it to the man. As soon as a subculture makes itself known, capitalism gobbles it up. Mass media brings the subculture into the public eye, and savvy retailers find ways to commercialize the subculture's signature look. People no longer have to painstakingly glue spikes onto a jacket if they want to be a punk for a day. They can hustle to a store and buy something straight off the rack. As the commercialization escalates, the subculture's original message gets watered down, and a style that once symbolized a lifestyle, ideology, or political stance becomes little more than a look. Before long, any challenge the subculture posed to the social order has disappeared into a palatable mix of price tags, caricatures, and radio hits. Buying a Sex Pistols T-shirt at Hot Topic—or runway-ready Vivienne Westwood leggings—is a far cry from supporting the idea that the English monarchy is a fascist regime.

Hebdige's theories focused on the styles of the 1970s and 80s, but the pattern of co-optation he described had already occurred earlier in the century with blue jeans. During the 1930s and 40s, counterculture creatives began wearing jeans; in the 50s, rebellious bikers and teenagers followed suit; and in the 60s, jeans were the garment of choice among New Left activists. In every instance, these groups opposed the dominant, middle-class American ideology and used jeans to set themselves apart from the mainstream.[39] But during the 1960s, large-scale sales and PR campaigns improved jeans' reputation. Apparel brands, fashion magazines, and popular entertainment convinced consumers that jeans were ideal garments not only for work but also for leisure, ease, comfort, and sociability. By the end of the decade, jeans had been thoroughly adopted by middle-class America and were making inroads across the globe.

Blue jeans shifted away from their status as contrarian garments to become egalitarian ones. No other article of clothing, advertisers argued, was as democratic, free, and unpretentious as a pair of blue jeans.[40] This new narrative emphasized jeans' classless nature and overrode the counter-cultural challenges leveled by activists, artists, and anarchists. Jeans became an article of clothing that could be worn by anyone and everyone without carrying the rebellious resonance that had made them popular in the first place.

The history of blue jeans can be read as a never-ending battle for social power. Once jeans hit the mainstream, individual subcultures began making their own signature styles. They faded, fringed, ripped, and embellished their jeans in an attempt to make a statement and reclaim some of denim's verve. High-end fashion responded with their own pre-worn jeans, co-opting the gritty look. Mass-market fashion then followed, making it impossible to distinguish between the jeans that had been torn as a sign of counter-cultural protest and those torn in the ever-forward march of capitalism. Finally, high fashion deemed the mainstream appropriations "tired" and "tacky," and shifted its attention elsewhere. In an endless cycle, denim trends have trickled down the line from intrepid avant-gardists to fashionistas to everyday people.

If Simmel were alive today, he would be able to dish up a hearty dose of "I told you so," because more than a century ago, he saw how this dynamic would play out. "Just as soon as the lower classes begin to copy [upper class] style," Simmel wrote, "the upper classes turn away from this style and adopt a new one, which in its turn differentiates them from the masses; and thus the game goes merrily on."[41]

And so the game did go on. By the early 2000s, designer jeans were sought after, and the coveted denim announced itself in a blaze of conspicuous glory. Swarovski crystal butterflies, rhinestone skulls, tiny cargo pockets, splashy logos, splattered paint, frayed edges, embroidered thighs, lace-up legs—if a bling-happy designer could imagine it, celebrities would wear it. A host of new premium brands like 7 for All Mankind, Rock and Republic, and True Religion hit luxury department stores. Embellished jeans weren't the product of a Saturday afternoon with a Bedazzler and iron-on patches; they were a clear status symbol.

Then the tide turned yet again. Once consumers could purchase gaudy jeans on every corner, high taste turned away from the "trashy" styles that had worked their way into mainstream closets. Savvy brands like A.P.C. positioned their jeans as artisanal goods, made with high quality materials and built to stand the test of time. In the 2010s, simple, dark wash skinny jeans stole the fashion spotlight, and "conscious products" and "sustainable practices" became buzzwords. While there are plenty of expensive jeans on the market today, most of them don't announce their designer quality as openly as the premium denim of the early 2000s. More affordable jeans made by brands like Frank and Oak, Everlane, and Madewell have simple, understated labels that inconspicuously grace the waistline, and some brands like Old Navy have forgone an exterior label altogether. Anonymous jeans didn't just become acceptable; they became fashionable.

While Simmel and Hebdige were both primarily concerned with the ways in which the back-and-forth movement of fashion pertains to class, blue jeans' pushmi-pullyu dynamic has extended to virtually every element of dominant culture. Gender, race, sexuality, and religion—they've all fallen into this characteristic to-and-fro pattern. For example, some conservative Muslim groups have deemed it haram for women to wear blue jeans, but millennial hijabsters (a portmanteau of hijabi and hipster) have made an art of looking fashionable in blue jeans and headscarves. This push and pull highlights a fact that fashion theorists have known for some time: clothing plays an integral role in the battle between social groups to establish, maintain, and expand dominance.[42]

Still, most fashion statements have a short-lived role to play in the warfare. They emerge with a bang, quickly become co-opted by the media and the market, and fade into anonymity. Consider Madonna's cone-bra, which no longer seems so scandalous. Or, going further back, one could point to the massive crinolines that caused a fuss in the mid-nineteenth century. But with blue jeans, we're still bouncing back-and-forth.

Most days, jeans are uncontroversial, normalized, egalitarian, and suitable for everyone. Yet, every now and then, a new trend emerges that jars the public out of complacency, as with ultra-low-rise Y2K jeans. But since 2017, it has seemed as if jarring jeans *are* the new trend. First, cut-out denim was all the rage. In more modest pairs, only the fabric around the pockets was cut out, but Google "extreme cut out jeans" or "invisible jeans" if you want to see how much fabric can be removed from a pair of jeans before it ceases to exist.

Subsequently, fashion designers and mass-market retailers have made a game out of which unexpected peekaboo they can play with next. Crotchless cut-out jeans, denim belts (legless jeans), and so-called "party in the back" jeans (designed to expose the wearer's buttock creases) have all caused internet sensations. Jean hotpants, which look more like denim bikini briefs, and detachable jeans offer full leg visibility. Chap jeans, whose legs are held up with thigh suspenders, and butt-zip jeans, which are exactly what they sound like, tend to offer a suggestion of access more than any real exposure.

The element of surprise in this new generation of jeans isn't always overtly sexual. Consider the mom jeans with clear plastic knees that made their way around the blog circuit in 2017, or Unravel Project's "inside out" jeans, which look like their wearer got lazy with the laundry. We also can't forget double- and triple-waisted jeans, which feature multiple beltlines and crotches.[43] In 2022, celebrities like Kim Kardashian and Julia Fox wore, arguably, the most modest denim surprise of all: "pantaboots," a $3,000 jean/boot combo that obviates the need choose the right footwear.

Men's fashion hasn't been immune from daring cuts, either. Spray-on jeans cling to every curve, and stacked jeans come with extra-long legs so the fabric can be bunched around the calves like leg warmers. Buzzy brand Y/Project has made a name off their unusual styles, including 2022's asymmetrical waist jeans, which feature four extra button holes on one side of the fly, and "lazy trousers," which look like lopsided, sagging trousers layered over fitted jeans. The offbeat Levi's x Vetements collaboration features a series of spliced, patchworked, zipped, and reworked garments, all of which look unsettlingly askew. Blue jeans are proof that, even when you think you've seen everything under the sun, there's still room for innovation.

Commenters have jeered at this increasing slate of "weird jeans," but these innovations couldn't be truer to denim's core values. Jeans have long been the territory of rebels, free-thinkers, and button-pushers. And these innovative cuts are nothing if not boundary-defying. Many of them fly in the face of traditional propriety, revealing hips, backs, and thighs. Even when the cut-away isn't particularly erotic, there's something uncanny about seeing skin in unexpected slivers, just as there's something equally unsettling about multiple waistbands, exposed hems, asymmetrical cuts, and a seamless pant/boot onesie. These jeans are disrupting social expectations in the same way that earlier generations of jeans pushed parents, schools, politicians, and media into moral panic. Nothing could be more blue jean than these garments' easy, in-your-face spirit.

A cynic might say that this new generation of jeans is a desperate byproduct of influencer culture. In a world saturated by images, the only way to compete for attention is to play a constant game of one-upmanship that can only culminate in ludicrous extremes. Because shoppers are willing to hop on the influencer bandwagon, mass-market retailers have decided they can turn a profit on trendy novelties. Moreover, those same retailers realize that if they're going to be major players, they need a panoply of options to keep consumers happy, and some of those options need to be distinctive. So much the better if those distinctive pieces garner a lot of press, as has been the case for "weird jeans" retailers like Topshop, ASOS, and Shein.

There's likely some truth to that position, but pure cynicism is too easy. We are also witnessing a culture hungry for play. By reinventing the most basic forms of clothing, designers and fashionistas are showing that they aren't taking anything in their wardrobes for granted. Even classics are fodder for experimentation—convention be damned. Everyone needs a little pleasure, drama, and effervescence in their life, and these norm-defying jeans embody the playful attitude that world-weary shoppers crave. We're seeing the pushmi spirit rush ahead, even if the mainstream pullyu stares aghast at the results.

In all likelihood, the pendulum will swing yet again once the zeitgeist changes. Classic shapes and minimal design will return. Maybe the subcultural passion for raw denim will become the next mainstream trend, or perhaps sizeless jeans will take the market by storm. Whatever the case may be, you can expect jeans to persist in their back-and-forth evolution. They will continue, by turns, to comfort and challenge us.

There's a kind of ideological restlessness at work in blue jeans. They carry so much meaning—and so many different meanings—for everyone who wears them, and as jeans have become more normalized across the globe, those meanings have only continued to multiply. For example, in 2021, the North Korean leader Kim Jong-un banned skinny jeans, which he considers a symbol of a "capitalistic lifestyle."[44] Clearly, blue jeans are still a potent cultural symbol. More than a century after they were created, the ideological battles surrounding them rage on. If anything, jeans have taken on more significance over time. And because virtually everyone knows of, wears, or wants blue jeans, the stakes of their symbolism have only gotten higher. What better place to struggle for ideological dominance than the most neutral battlefield—the non-place of fashion?

CONCLUSION

THE PARADOX
OF JEANS

When I was first introduced to the work of the French anthropologist Claude Lévi-Strauss in college, all I could think about was blue jeans. The only association I had with that particular combination of names was a little red tab jutting out from a pocket. But by the time I finished graduate school, I couldn't look at a pair of Levi's without thinking about Lévi-Strauss and structural anthropology. It was more than the kismet of their names, although I now think of the similarity as one of history's quirky jokes. Claude Lévi-Strauss offered me a new way to think about blue jeans with his theory of binary opposition.

Hot; cold. Black; white. Good; evil. Male; female. Urban; rural. Strong; weak. Light; dark. Left; right. Nurture; nature. The list of familiar opposites goes on and on. Lévi-Strauss argued that the prevalence of these binaries isn't because salt is, in some objective reality, the opposite of pepper. ("What about us?" cumin, coriander, and a whole rack of other spices wail.) Instead, Lévi-Strauss claimed, the structure of the human mind compels us to create opposites in order to make sense of the world. This tendency is so hard-wired that humans readily apply binaries even when clear-cut oppositions may not truly exist. Consider: at what point does short become tall? When does a lukewarm latte become cold, and how does it compare to an iced latte that's grown warm? Or, to put it in more Lévi-Straussian terms, the line between "raw" and "cooked" is not as evident as it may initially seem.

If one were to ponder how humans categorize the world, one could immediately point to a number of instances where someone is neither good nor evil, thick nor thin, jaw-droppingly gorgeous nor monstrously hideous. We live with in-betweens daily. Yet, we still spend a large portion of our lives classifying people and objects by simple opposites.

Binary thinking is often reductive, but it isn't inherently bad. According to Lévi-Strauss, binaries are the necessary building blocks of all human thought and classification. Everyone everywhere structures their world with binary pairs because contrast is how we find meaning. I know that billionaires are rich because they aren't poor, and I know that minimum-wage workers are poor because they aren't rich. The meaning comes not from the individual terms but from the contrast. Ideally binary oppositions are just the starting place for human thought, not its totality. Still, it's hard to deny how easily dichotomies, dualities, pairs, and opposites can suck us in. Gut-reactions often veer toward these hard lines of thinking. Is this person a friend or foe? Am I making a good or bad first impression? The more basic, immediate, and reactive a thought, the more likely it is to be premised on a binary.

If Lévi-Strauss convinced me of the importance of binary thinking, blue jeans have taught me how rich those binaries can be. How can a single garment contain so many opposing values? Are blue jeans casual or catwalk-ready? Ordinary or transgressive? Durable or disposable? Sexy or slouchy? Masculine or feminine? Timeless or trendy? Global or regional? Normcore or distinctive? Liberating or confining? Meaningful or meaningless?

The answer is, quite simply, yes. They are all of these things. And that's where their fascination lies. When one takes all of blue jeans' binary oppositions into account and places the contradictions side by side, it's possible to see jeans in a new light. It's evident that even the most basic objects can become battlegrounds for opposing meanings. Every time one group of people uses blue jeans a certain way, another group reacts and uses them in the opposite manner. Over time, this back-and-forth has given blue jeans such a wide array of meanings that humans have come to take the complex tangle for granted. We go about our daily lives, acting as if a garment that means everything in fact means nothing.

In a sense, this assumption is true. When a single object symbolizes so many conflicting ideas, emotions, and purposes, it almost ceases to represent any of them.

Blue jeans, as a cultural object, are up for grabs. They've become a universal signifier, so crammed with meaning they're practically invisible. Still, it would be wonderful if we could start seeing jeans again. Because the more often people recognize the meaning in the objects they take for granted, the more they can appreciate those objects' power.

I recently saw jeans again, in a new and unexpected way. While I was writing this book, my family had to place my paternal grandmother into hospice care for renal failure. During one of our visits, I told Nanny what I was working on, and she lit up. "I used to work at Blue Buckle," she revealed. "I did the pockets." I had always been close to my grandmother, but I had never known that she spent several years inside that imposing brick warehouse, laying out cloth and inserting rivets. It wasn't a glamorous place to work, but Nanny had fond memories of her time there. Not of the monotonous labor or the hot factory floor, but of the people. Of the managers and coworkers she cut up with at lunchtime. Of the other pocket layers who talked with her about motherhood and children.

For as long as I can remember, my grandmother was a lover of flashy jewelry, and she never missed a chance to dress up. Her favorite boutique was called Dressin' Gaudy, and one of her prized possessions was a puffy-armed beaver-fur coat. But in her last moments, Nanny rejected such extravagance. She left behind meticulous instructions for her funeral and stressed multiple times that it should be a casual dress event. She wanted her funeral to feel easy, simple, and honest. She wanted people to be comfortable with her passing and to feel free to express themselves as they would in their daily lives. So, as Nanny was escorted to her final resting place, she was accompanied by six pallbearers, all of whom wore blue jeans.

That's a powerful sentiment for a few yards of blue cloth. And yet, if I stop and think about it, perhaps there is nothing more powerful than the things that seem most ordinary. Humans *need* ordinary. We need things that will comfort us and give stability. Adventure is thrilling, but without the ordinary things in our lives there to ground us, it would be all too easy to spin off our axes. By definition, humans take ordinary things for granted, yet ordinariness is one of the most complex components of human existence. Everything ordinary carries unspoken volumes about the norms, cultural expectations, and desires that guide our lives. The things that each person, society, or culture accepts as ordinary are the very things that define them. And suddenly we're back to Lévi-Strauss' baffling binaries. At what point do the most ordinary objects take on extraordinary significance?

Few objects seem more ordinary than blue jeans. In their purest terms, jeans are nothing more than two denim tubes and a crotch. Yet, they contain multitudes. They show us history's good and bad sides. They reveal the difficult balance that people of different beliefs, races, cultures, genders, and classes strike between domination and subservience. They illustrate how those struggles manifest in the material goods we keep in our closets and wear on our bodies. Blue jeans are far more than a mirror reflecting the values people hold. Instead, they actively help create those values, reproduce them, and spread them around the globe.

NOTES

Introduction

1 Catherine Salfino, "Innovation and Culture Shifts Drive Increases in Global Denim," *Sourcing Journal,* August 1, 2018, https://sourcingjournal.com/topics/lifestyle-monitor/global-denim-innovation-113793/.

2 "Denim Jeans Market Size, Share & Trends Analysis Report by End User (Children, Men, Women), by Sales Channel (Offline, Online), by Region (North America, APAC, Europe, MEA), and Segment Forecasts, 2019 – 2025," Grand View Research, August 2019, accessed April 8, 2021, https://www.grandviewresearch.com/industry-analysis/denim-jeans-market.

3 "Denim in 2022: What Will Global Consumers Want?" Cotton Incorporated *Lifestyle Monitor*, December 6, 2021, https://lifestylemonitor.cottoninc.com/denim-in-2022/.

4 Ibid.

5 Yves St. Laurent et al, *Yves St. Laurent: The Metropolitan Museum of Art, New York* (London: Thames and Hudson, 1983), 23.

6 "Straight-Fit Jeans in Dirty Winter Blue Denim," Saint Laurent, accessed January 7, 2022, https://www.ysl.com/en-us/straight -fit-jeans-in-dirty-winter-blue-denim-809466854.html.

7 Tanisha C. Ford, "SNCC Women, Denim, and the Politics of Dress," *The Journal of Southern History* 79, no. 3 (2013): 625-58, accessed April 8, 2021, http://www.jstor.org/stable/23795090.

Chapter 1

1 The "guy" in question was probably Michael Allen Harris. You can read about him here: Michael Allen Harris, "Experience: I Mine for 100-Year-Old Jeans," *The Guardian*, September 25, 2015, https://www.theguardian.com/lifeandstyle/2015/sep/25/ experience-i-mine-for-denim.

2 "History of the Levi's® 501® Jeans," Levi Strauss, accessed July 10, 2021, https://www.levistrauss.com/wp-content/uploads /2014/01/History-of-Levis-501-Jeans.pdf.

3 "Jean," *Oxford English Dictionary* Online, December 2021 (Oxford University Press), accessed January 4, 2022, https:// www.oed.com/view/Entry/100960.

4 James Sullivan, *Jeans: A Cultural History of an American Icon* (New York: Gotham, 2006), 13-14.

5 Bethanne Patrick and John Thompson, *An Uncommon History of Common Things* (National Geographic, 2009), 160.

6 David Coles, *Chromatopia: An Illustrated History of Color* (New York: Thames and Hudson, 2018), 127.

7 Ibid., 35.

8   Jenny Balfour-Paul, *Indigo: Egyptian Mummies to Blue Jeans* (Buffalo, NY: Firefly Books, 2012), 33.

9   Ibid., 34-37.

10 Coles, *Chromatopia,* 65.

11 Ibid., 35.

12 "Blue—Blues," *Dictionary of Traded Goods and Commodities, 1550-1820* (University of Wolverhampton, 2007), accessed April 8, 2021, https://www.british-history.ac.uk/no-series/traded-goods-dictionary/1550-1820/blue-blues.

13 Michel Pastoureau, *Blue: The History of a Color,* trans. Markus I. Cruse (Princeton: Princeton University Press, 2002), 123.

14 Balfour-Paul, *Indigo,* 71.

15 John S. Farmer, *Slang and Its Analogues Past and Present,* vol. 1 (London: 1890), 252.

16 Ibid.

17 Abigail Cain, "Why Blue Is the World's Favorite Color," *Artsy,* August 29, 2017, https://www.artsy.net/article/artsy-editorial-blue-worlds-favorite-color.

18 Ibid.

19 Pastoureau, *Blue,* 180.

20 Arabella Youens, "Why 'Blue and Green Should Never Be Seen' Is Outdated, Absurd, and Just Plain Wrong," *Country Life*, July 26, 2021, https://www.countrylife.co.uk/interiors/why-blue-and-green-should-never-be-seen-is-outdated-absurd-and-just-plain-wrong-230477.

21 Jeffrey C. Splitstoser et al, "Early Pre-Hispanic Use of Indigo Blue in Peru," *Science Advances 2*, no. 9 (September 2016), doi: 10.1126/sciadv.1501623.

22 Balfour-Paul, *Indigo,* 19.

23 Catherine E. McKinley, *Indigo: In Search of the Color that Seduced the World* (New York: Bloomsbury, 2012), 230-231.

24 Coles, *Chromatopia*, 43.

25 Balfour-Paul, *Indigo*, 121-122.

26 Ibid., 102.

27 Ibid., 109-111.

28 John Bullokar, *An English Expositor, Teaching the Interpretation of the Hardest Words Used in Our Language* (London, 1616); quoted in David Scott Kastan, with Stephen Farthing, *On Color* (New Haven: Yale University Press, 2018), 124.

29 Balfour-Paul, *Indigo*, 56; Sullivan, *Jeans*, 21.

30 Sven Beckert, *Empire of Cotton: A Global History* (New York: Vintage, 2014), xv; Ibid., 30.

31 Ibid., 51.

32 E.W. L. Tower, quoted in Subhas Bhattacharya, "The Indigo Revolt of Bengal," *Social Scientist* 5, no. 12 (July 1777): 13.

33 Andrea Feeser, *Red, White, and Black Make Blue: Indigo in the Fabric of Colonial South Carolina Life* (Athens, GA: University of Georgia Press, 2013), 16.

34 Ibid., 17-23.

35 Ibid., 45.

36 Kastan and Farthing, *On Color*, 126.

37 Colesworthy Grant, *Rural Life in Bengal*, 2nd ed. (London: W. Thacker & Co., 1866), 87.

38 Terence R. Blackburn, *A Miscellany of Mutinies and Massacres in India* (New Delhi: APH Publishing, 2007), 161.

39 Bhattacharya, "Indigo Revolt," 16.

40 Grant, *Rural Life,* 90.

41 Bhattacharya, "Indigo Revolt," 13.

42 Ibid., 16.

43 George Watt, *Pamphlet on Indigo*, (n.p., [1890s]), 15.

44 Balfour-Paul, *Indigo*, 75.

45 Ibid., 82.

46 Rachel Louise Snyder, *Fugitive Denim: A Moving Story of People and Pants in the Borderless World of Global Trade* (New York: W. W. Norton, 2009), 149.

47 "Reasons to Celebrate: 148 Years of the Denim Blue Jean," Cotton Incorporated *Lifestyle Monitor*, accessed June 25, 2021, https://lifestylemonitor.cottoninc.com/reasons-to -celebrate/.

48 "Denim in 2022: What Will Global Consumers Want?" Cotton Incorporated *Lifestyle Monitor*, December 6, 2021, https://lifestylemonitor.cottoninc.com/denim-in-2022/.

49 Tatiana Schlossberg, *Inconspicuous Consumption: The Environmental Impact You Don't Know You Have* (New York: Hachette, 2019), 136.

50 Snyder, *Fugitive Denim*, 118.

51 Ibid., 130.

52 Ibid., 119-120.

53 "Xintang Pays Heavy Price for Putting World in Blue Jeans," *China Daily USA*, July 31, 2017, https://www.chinadaily.com .cn/kindle/2017-07/31/content_30305246.htm.

54 Guang Li, Mingzhuo Jiang, and Guang Lu, "The Denim Capital of the World Is So Polluted You Can't Give the Houses Away," China Dialogue, August 13, 2013, https://

chinadialogue.net/en/pollution/6283-the-denim-capital-of
-the-world-so-polluted-you-can-t-give-the-houses-away/.

55 "The Dirty Secret Behind Jeans and Bras," Greenpeace,
December 1, 2010, accessed June 25, 2021, http://web.archive
.org/web/20110312074819/http://www.greenpeace.org/
eastasia/news/textile-pollution-xintang-gurao/.

56 Li, Jiang, and Lu, "The Denim Capital of the World."

57 Krista Mahr, "China's Textile Industry: How Dirty Are Your
Jeans?" *Time,* November 30, 2010, https://science.time.com
/2010/11/30/chinas-textile-industry-how-dirty-are-your
-jeans/.

58 Snyder, *Fugitive Denim,* 135-136.

59 Jessica Liu, "Where Will Xintang Jeans Move Next?" *DC,*
February 12, 2018, https://www.cndc.co/where-will-xintang
-jeans-move-to-in-2018/.

60 Snyder, *Fugitive Denim,* 77.

61 "Chemists Go Green to Make Better Blue Jeans," *Nature* 553,
no. 128 (January 9, 2018), doi: https://doi.org/10.1038/d41586
-018-00103-8.

62 Emily Matchar, "Have Scientists Found a Greener Way to
Make Blue Jeans?" *Smithsonian Mag,* January 22, 2018,
https://www.smithsonianmag.com/innovation/have-scientists
-found-greener-way-to-make-blue-jeans-180967902/.

63 Ibid.

64 Levi's®, "The 501® Jean: Stories of an Original — Full
Documentary," YouTube video, 18:01, March 16, 2016, accessed
July 8, 2021, https://www.youtube.com/watch?v=6R9cAoCyatA.

65 Aims McGuinness, *Path of Empire: Panama and the California
Gold Rush* (Ithaca: Cornell University Press, 2008), 4-6.

66 Lynn Downey, *Levi Strauss: The Man Who Gave Blue Jeans to the World* (Amherst: University of Massachusetts, 2016), 113-114.

67 Ibid., 114.

68 Jacob Davis to Levi Strauss, July 5, 1872; quoted in Downey, *Levi Strauss,* 116.

69 "History of the Levi's® 501® Jeans."

70 Sullivan, *Jeans,* 110-111.

71 Sandra Curtis Comstock, "The Making of an American Icon: The Transformation of Blue Jeans During the Great Depression," *Global Denim,* ed. Daniel Miller and Sophie Woodward (Oxford: Berg, 2011), 32.

72 Ibid., 38.

73 Ibid., 26.

74 Tracey Panek, "Throwback Thursday: Celebrating 80 Years of Women's Jeans," Levi Strauss, September 4, 2014, https://www.levistrauss.com/2014/09/04/celebrating-80-years-of-womens-jeans/.

75 Jeremy Agnew, *The Old West in Fact and Film: History Versus Hollywood* (Jefferson, NC: McFarland and Company, 2012), 126.

76 Comstock, "The Making of an American Icon," 36.

77 Donald Worster, *Dust Bowl: The Southern Plains in the 1930s* (Oxford: Oxford University Press, 1979), 49.

78 Comstock, "The Making of an American Icon," 36.

79 Ibid., 38.

80 Henrik Vejlgaard, *The Lifestyle Puzzle: Who We Are in the 21st Century* (Amherst, NY: Prometheus, 2010), 186.

81 Snyder, *Fugitive Denim,* 161.

Chapter 2

1   Roberta Sassatelli, "Indigo Bodies: Fashion, Mirror Work, and Sexual Identity in Milan," *Global Denim,* eds. Daniel Miller and Sophie Woodward (Oxford: Berg, 2011), 131.

2   Hanna Flanagan, "Why Are GenZ TikTokers Making Fun of Skinny Jeans and Side Parts? Everything You Need to Know," *People*, February 18, 2021, https://people.com/style/gen-z-tiktokers-slam-millennials-side-parts-and-skinny-jeans/.

3   "Denim in 2022: What Will Global Consumers Want?" Cotton Incorporated *Lifestyle Monitor*, December 6, 2021, https://lifestylemonitor.cottoninc.com/denim-in-2022/.

4   James Sullivan, *Jeans: A Cultural History of an American Icon* (New York: Gotham Books, 2006), 83.

5   Ed Cray, *Levi's* (Boston: Houghton Mifflin, 1978), 110.

6   Ibid., 112.

7   Sullivan, *Jeans,* 85.

8   "When Denim Was Dangerous," Levi Strauss and Company, March 28, 2014, https://www.levistrauss.com/2014/03/28/when-denim-was-dangerous/.

9   Cray, *Levi's,* 150.

10 Tanisha C. Ford, "SNCC Women, Denim, and the Politics of Dress," *The Journal of Southern History* 79, no. 3 (August 2013): 626.

11 Ibid., 631-632.

12 Ibid., 627.

13 Ibid.

14 Juliane Fürst, *Flowers through Concrete: Explorations in Soviet Hippieland* (Oxford: Oxford University Press, 2021), 310.

15 Alexéi Rudevich and Russkaya Semyorka, "Worth Going to Prison For: Getting Hold of Jeans in the USSR," *Russia Beyond*, September 16, 2014, https://www.rbth.com/arts/2014/09/16/worth_going_to_prison_for_getting_hold_of_jeans_in_the_ussr_39833.html.

16 Ibid.

17 Tracey Panek, "Blue Jeans and the Fall of the Berlin Wall," Levi Strauss and Company, November 7, 2019, https://www.levistrauss.com/2019/11/07/blue-jeans-and-the-fall-of-the-berlin-wall/.

18 Régis Debray, *Manifestes médiologiques* (Paris: Gallimard, 1994), 135.

19 David Shuck, "Remembering Belarus's Denim Revolution," Heddel's, August 25, 2014, updated May 9, 2018, https://www.heddels.com/2014/08/remembering-belaruss-denim-revolution/.

20 Margot Letain, "The 'Denim Revolution': A Glass Half Full," *Open Democracy*, April 10, 2006, https://www.opendemocracy.net/en/denim_3441jsp/.

21 Charlotte Sector, "Belarusians Wear Jeans in Silent Protest," *ABC News*, February 4, 2006, https://abcnews.go.com/International/story?id=1502762.

22 Ibid.

23 Shivani Azad, "Shocked to See Women in Ripped Jeans, What Message Are They Sending to Society: Uttarakhand CM Tirath Singh Rawat," *The Times India,* March 17, 2021, https://timesofindia.indiatimes.com/city/dehradun/shocked-to-see-women-in-ripped-jeans-what-message-are-they-sending-to-society-ukhand-cm/articleshow/81537465.cms.

24 *India Today* Web Desk, "Uttarakhand CM Tirath Rawat Ripped Over Ripped Jeans Remark: All You Need to

Know," *India Today*, March 19, 2021, https://www
.indiatoday.in/india/story/tirath-rawat-ripped-jeans
-controversy-all-you-need-to-know-1781166-2021-03-19.

25 Azad, "Shocked to See Women in Ripped Jeans."

26 Press Trust of India, "Tirath Singh Rawat Apologises for
Ripped Jeans Remark but Says Wearing Torn Jeans 'Not Right,'"
India Today, March 20, 2021, https://www.indiatoday.in/india/
story/tirath-singh-rawat-apologises-ripped-jeans-remark-says
-wearing-torn-jeans-not-right-1781449-2021-03-20.

27 *India Today* Web Desk, "Uttarakhand CM Tirath Rawat Ripped."

28 Kristen Bateman, "The 10 TikTok Subcultures Shaping
Fashion Right Now," *W Magazine,* January 27, 2021,
https://www.wmagazine.com/fashion/tiktok-fashion
-trends-subcultures-goths.

29 "Subcultures Are the New Demographics," TikTok for
Business, May 20, 2021, https://www.tiktok.com/business/
en-US/blog/subcultures-are-the-new-demographics.

30 Ken Gelder, "The Field of Subcultural Studies," *The
Subcultures Reader*, 2nd ed., ed. Ken Gelder (New York:
Routledge, 2005), 1.

31 Fürst, *Flowers through Concrete*, 310.

32 Lauraine Leblanc, *Pretty in Punk: Girls' Gender Resistance
in a Boys' Subculture* (New Brunswick, NJ: Rutgers
University Press, 1999), 4.

33 Marcia A. Morgado, "Uncovered Butts and Recovered Rules:
Sagging Pants and the Logic of Abductive Inference," *The
Meanings of Dress,* 4th ed., eds. Kimberly A. Miller Spillman
and Andrew Reilly (New York: Fairchild Books, 2019), 19.

34 Ibid.

35 Niko Koppel, "Are Your Jeans Sagging? Go Directly to Jail," *New York Times,* August 30, 2007, https://www.nytimes.com/2007/08/30/fashion/30baggy.html.

36 Shahid Abdul-Karim, "For Some, Sagging Pants Can Carry Greater Meaning," *Washington Times,* July 13, 2014, https://www.washingtontimes.com/news/2014/jul/13/for-some-sagging-pants-carry-greater-meaning/.

37 Koppel, "Are Your Jeans Sagging?"

38 Abdul-Karim, "For Some, Sagging Pants Can Carry Greater Meaning."

39 "Where Are They Now? JNCO Jeans," *Highsnobiety*, March 16, 2020, https://www.highsnobiety.com/p/jnco-history/.

40 Zachary Crockett, "JNCO, the Terrible Jeans Brand from the '90s, Finally Goes Out of Business," *The Hustle*, February 21, 2018, https://thehustle.co/jnco-jeans-goes-bankrupt/.

41 Leonora Epstein, "11 Reasons You Used to Wear JNCO Jeans," *BuzzFeed*, June 6, 2013, https://www.buzzfeed.com/amphtml/leonoraepstein/reasons-you-used-to-wear-jnco-jeans.

42 Elizabeth M. Matelski, *Reducing Bodies: Mass Culture and the Female Figure in Postwar America* (New York: Routledge, 2017), 17.

43 "Our Guide to Shopping Unisex," Levi's, June 2020, https://www.levi.com/US/en_US/blog/article/our-guide-to-shopping-unisex/.

44 Ashley Fetters, "Toward a Universal Theory of 'Mom Jeans,'" *The Atlantic,* August 28, 2019, https://www.theatlantic.com/family/archive/2019/08/how-mom-jeans-became-cool-again/596992/.

45   Eloise R. Germic, Stine Eckert, and Fred Vultee, "The Impact of Instagram Mommy Blogger Content on the Perceived Self-Efficacy of Mothers," *Social Media + Society* (July 2021), https://doi.org/10.1177/20563051211041649.

46   Robin Givhan, "Can Obama Elevate the Look of Presidential Downtime? We Can Only Hope," *Washington Post*, July 26, 2009, https://www.washingtonpost.com/wp-dyn/content/article/2009/07/23/AR2009072304042.html?wprss=rss_print/style.

47   Eliana Dockterman, "One Size Fits None," *Time,* accessed October 18, 2021, https://time.com/how-to-fix-vanity-sizing/.

48   Kate Hardcastle, "Marilyn Monroe's Dress Size Myth: Why Fashion Must Size Up," *Forbes*, July 7, 2021, https://www.forbes.com/sites/katehardcastle/2021/07/07/marilyn-monroes-dress-size-myth-why-fashion-must-size-up/?sh=65413b840c9c.

49   Roger Dooley, "The Psychology of Vanity Sizing," *Forbes*, July 29, 2013, https://www.forbes.com/sites/rogerdooley/2013/07/29/vanity-sizing/?sh=509c2b9f1e32.

50   Daniel Miller and Sophie Woodward, *Blue Jeans: The Art of the Ordinary* (Berkeley: University of California Press, 2012), 49.

51   Abram Sauer, "Are Your Pants Lying to You? An Investigative Report," *Esquire,* September 7, 2010, https://www.esquire.com/style/mens-fashion/a8386/pants-size-chart-090710/.

52   Maria Cristina Pavarini, "Jeans of the Future: One Size Fits All," *The Spin Off*, June 17, 2021, https://www.the-spin-off.com/news/stories/The-Trends-Jeans-of-the-future-One-size-fits-all-15967; "Sene x Emma," Sene Studio, https://senestudio.com/collections/emma.

53 Paceysgirls, "1980 Calvin Klein Jeans Commercial feat. Brooke Shields," YouTube video, 1:03, uploaded August 9, 2008, accessed October 5, 2021, https://www.youtube.com/watch?v =AXzR5b6HoIA.

54 Shakuntala Banaji, "Loving with Irony: Young Bombay Viewers Discuss Clothing, Sex, and Their Encounters with Media," *Sex Education* 6, no. 4 (2006): 377-391, accessed through London School of Economics Research Online, http://eprints.lse.ac.uk/27015/, 8. Emphasis in original.

55 Davesshindig, "Karen Ferrari Sexy Calvin Klein Jeans Commercial BANNED!" YouTube video, 0:30, uploaded February 15, 2012, accessed October 5, 2021, https://www .youtube.com/watch?v=ksxH0FDGUnU.

56 Rachel A. Van Cleave, "Sex, Lies, and Honor in Italian Rape Law," *Suffolk University Law Review* 38, no. 427 (January 2005): 446, https://ssrn.com/abstract=2083776.

57 Ibid., 447.

58 Corte Suprema di Cassazione, Session 3 (November 6, 1998), Cristiano, *Il Foro Italiano* II, CXXII (1999), 163; quoted in Van Cleave, "Sex, Lies, and Honor," 448.

59 Van Cleave, "Sex, Lies, and Honor," 448.

60 Ibid., 450.

61 "Italians Protest Rape Ruling," *CBS News*, February 12, 1999, https://www.cbsnews.com/news/italians-protest-rape-ruling/.

62 Alessandra Stanley, "Ruling on Tight Jeans and Rape Sets Off Anger in Italy," *New York Times,* February 16, 1999, https:// www.nytimes.com/1999/02/16/world/ruling-on-tight-jeans -and-rape-sets-off-anger-in-italy.html.

63 Ibid.

64 "Why Denim?" Denim Day Info, accessed October 5, 2021, https://www.denimdayinfo.org/why-denim.

65 Corte Suprema di Cassazione, Session 3 (November 26, 2001), Akid, n.42289/2001, available at www.cittadinolex.kataweb.it/Article/ O,IS19,IS793/1,00.html; quoted in Van Cleave, "Sex, Lies, and Honor," 452.

Chapter 3

1 Marc Augé, *Non-Places: An Introduction to Supermodernity,* trans. John Howe (London: Verso, 2008), viii.

2 Ibid., xii.

3 Wan Nur Syaza Sahira Wan Rusli et al, "Intra and Intersentential Code-Switching Phenomena in Modern Malay Songs," *Southeast Asian Journal of English Language Studies* 24, no. 3 (September 2018), doi: 10.17576/3L-2018-2403-14, 185; Ainaa Aiman, "KRU on the Upbeat, from Hip Hop to Music Mogul," *Free Malaysia Today,* March 23, 2021, https://www.freemalaysiatoday.com/category/leisure/2021/03/23/kru-on-the-upbeat-from-hip-hop-to-music-mogul.

4 W. David Marx, *Ametora: How Japan Saved American Style* (New York: Basic Books, 2015), 76.

5 Ibid., 24.

6 Ibid., 78-79.

7 Ibid., xv.

8 Daniel Miller, "The Limits of Jeans in Kannur, Kerala," in *Global Denim,* eds. Daniel Miller and Sophie Woodward (Oxford: Berg, 2011), 87.

9 "Denim Is Adapting and Evolving: Surviving in a World of Athleisure Influence," Cotton Incorporated *Lifestyle Monitor*, accessed September 9, 2021, https://lifestylemonitor.cottoninc.com/denim-is-adapting-evolving/.

10 "Preparing for a Comeback: The Blue Jean," Cotton Incorporated *Lifestyle Monitor*, accessed September 9, 2021, https://lifestylemonitor.cottoninc.com/preparing-for-a-comeback/.

11 Ibid.

12 Ibid.

13 Miller, "The Limits of Jeans," 90; Ibid., 95.

14 Clare M. Wilkinson-Weber, "Diverting Denim: Screening Jeans in Bollywood," in *Global Denim,* eds. Daniel Miller and Sophie Woodward (Oxford: Berg, 2011), 51.

15 "The Arvind Story," Arvind, accessed September 23, 2021, https://www.arvind.com/arvind-story.

16 Haley Nahman, "Is Denim in an Identity Crisis?" *New York Times,* November 10, 2021, https://www.nytimes.com/2021/11/10/style/denim-jeans-trends.html.

17 Ibid.

18 Ibid.

19 Niall Ferguson, *Civilization: The West and the Rest* (New York: Penguin Books, 2012), 240; via Nahman, "Is Denim in an Identity Crisis?"

20 "Denim Is Adapting and Evolving," Cotton Incorporated *Lifestyle Monitor*.

21 "Denim in 2022: What Will Global Customers Want?" Cotton Incorporated *Lifestyle Monitor*, accessed January 20, 2022, https://lifestylemonitor.cottoninc.com/denim-in-2022/.

22 "Wrangler Pleated Barrel Cord Jeans," Free People, accessed January 20, 2022, https://www.freepeople.com/shop/wrangler -pleated-barrel-cord-jeans/; Perrie Samotin, "Topshop Is Now Selling See-Through Plastic Jeans," *Glamour,* April 24, 2017, https://www.glamour.com/story/topshop-clear -see-through-plastic-jeans; "Rubber Jeans Lace Up Sides," Invincible Rubber, accessed February 15, 2022, https://www .invinciblerubber.com/rubber-jeans-lace-up-sides.

23 Bianca Betancourt, "Justin Timberlake Wants the Internet to Forget About His Double-Denim Moment with Britney Spears," *Harper's Bazaar*, February 2, 2021, https://www .harpersbazaar.com/celebrity/latest/a35394165/justin -timberlake-talks-double-denim-britney-spears-moment/.

24 Georg Simmel, "Fashion," *American Journal of Sociology* 62, no. 6 (1957): 541–58, http://www.jstor.org/stable/2773129.

25 Michael Shawn Malone, *Bill and Dave: How Hewlett and Packard Built the World's Greatest Company* (New York: Portfolio, 2007), 132.

26 Megan Garber, "Casual Friday and the 'End of the Office Dress Code,'" *The Atlantic,* May 25, 2016, https://www .theatlantic.com/entertainment/archive/2016/05/casual-friday -and-the-end-of-the-office-dress-code/484334/.

27 Ibid.

28 "Casual Workplaces: Why Every Denim Brand Benefits," Cotton Incorporated *Lifestyle Monitor*, March 23, 2020, https://lifestylemonitor.cottoninc.com/casual-workplaces/.

29 Joan DeJean, *The Age of Comfort: When Paris Discovered Casual—and the Modern Home Began* (New York: Bloomsbury, 2009), 50-51.

30 Ibid., 186.

31 Daniel Roche, *A History of Everyday Things: The Birth of Consumption in France, 1600-1800* (Cambridge: Cambridge University Press, 2000), 129.

32 Witold Rybczynski, *Home: A Short History of an Idea* (New York: Viking, 1986), 220.

33 Deirdre Clemente, "Why and When Did Americans Begin to Dress So Casually?" *Time,* August 5, 2015, https://time.com /3984690/american-casual-dressing/.

34 Christina Binkley, "The Relentless Rise of Power Jeans," *Wall Street Journal,* November 6, 2009, https://www.wsj.com/ articles/SB10001424052748703574604574501463104873016.

35 Muireann Carey-Campbell, "Casual Dress Has Gone Global," *New York Times,* February 3, 2014, https://www.nytimes.com/ roomfordebate/2014/02/03/the-casual-couture-of-the-average -american/casual-dress-has-gone-global.

36 Simmel, "Fashion," 542-544.

37 Christian Allaire, "Get to Know South Africa's Coolest Denim Line," *Vogue,* June 23, 2020, https://www.vogue.com/article/ tshepo-jeans-south-africa-denim-line.

38 Dick Hebdige, *Subculture: The Meaning of Style* (New York: Routledge, 1979), 132.

39 Malcolm Barnard, *Fashion as Communication,* 2nd ed. (New York: Routledge, 1996), 273.

40 Fred Davis, *Fashion, Culture and Identity* (Chicago: University of Chicago Press, 1992), 70-71.

41 Simmel, "Fashion," 545.

42 Barnard, *Fashion as Communication,* 97.

43 Lauren Sharkey, "Rips, Zips, and Invisible Jeans: The Most Bizarre New Denim Trends," *Yahoo! Life*, December 18, 2017, https://www.yahoo.com/lifestyle/rips-slits-invisible-jeans-most-slideshow-wp-115314380.html.

44 Priya Elan, "North Korea Bans Skinny Jeans as Symbol of 'Capitalistic Lifestyle,'" *The Guardian*, May 26, 2021, https://www.theguardian.com/fashion/2021/may/26/north-korea-bans-skinny-jeans.

INDEX